THE TIK-TOK MAN OF OZ

Performance Script

Book and Lyrics by L. Frank Baum

Music by Louis F. Gottschalk

Additional songs by
Oliver Morosco and Victor L. Schertzinger
and Flora Wulschner, Eugene Cowles, Paul West, and Safford Waters

Abridgement by Eric Shanower

A VINTAGE BROADWAY BOOK

The Tik-Tok Man of Oz Performance Script
Published by Hungry Tiger Press
314 SE 129th Avenue
Portland, OR 97233
www.hungrytigerpress.com

ISBN 978-1-929527-28-1

Also available from Hungry Tiger Press:
The Tik-Tok Man of Oz Piano-Vocal Score (ISBN 978-1-929527-30-4)
All Wound Up: The Making of The Tik-Tok Man of Oz (ISBN 978-1-929527-29-8)

THE TIK-TOK MAN OF OZ

Principal Roles

BETSY BOBBIN, female, Soprano – girl from Oklahoma, innocent but no-nonsense

HANK THE MULE, animal impersonator role, non-singing – Betsy's pet

SHAGGY MAN, male, Baritone/Tenor – amiable tramp from Colorado in search of his long-lost brother, takes life as it comes

OZMA THE ROSE PRINCESS, female, Soprano II – fairy princess who longs to be restored to the kingdom that cast her out, in love with Private Files

POLYCHROME THE RAINBOW'S DAUGHTER, female, Soprano II – rainbow fairy fallen from her bow to wander the cold earth, but happy to flirt with Ruggedo the Metal Monarch

TIK-TOK THE CLOCKWORK MAN, male, Baritone – mechanical man wound up with a key, ever ready to render faithful service as long as he doesn't run down

QUEEN ANN OF OOGABOO, female, Soprano II – battle-axe out to conquer the world with her small army, and in search of a husband

PRIVATE FILES, male, Baritone/Tenor – reluctant soldier and incurable romantic, more interested in wooing Ozma the Rose Princess than in fighting

RUGGEDO THE METAL MONARCH, male, Bass – blustery ruler of an underground kingdom, filled with rage toward surface-dwellers, but with a soft spot for Polychrome the Rainbow's Daughter

Minor Roles

MOSS ROSE
JACQUE ROSE
ROYAL GARDENER
MESSENGER OF THE ROSE KINGDOM
UGLY MAN

Also WAVES, ROSES, RAINBOW GIRLS,
ARMY OF OOGABOO, FIELD FLOWERS, *and* METAL IMPS

MUSICAL NUMBERS

1 – Overture – The Tik-Tok Man of Oz "Selection" (Gottschalk)

2 – Prelude – "A Storm at Sea" – Dance of WAVES (Gottschalk)

ACT ONE

3 – "An Apple's the Cause of It All" – SHAGGY MAN (Baum/Gottschalk)

4 – "The Magnet of Love" – BETSY (Baum/Gottschalk)

5 – "Oh! My Bow" with Dance of the Rainbows – POLYCHROME with RAIN-BOW GIRLS (Baum/Gottschalk)

6 – "I Want to Be Somebody's Girlie" - POLYCHROME (Schertzinger)

7 – "The Clockwork Man" – TIK-TOK with CHORUS (Baum/Gottschalk)

8 – "The Army of Oogaboo" – QUEEN ANN, FILES, and the ARMY OF OOGABOO (Baum/Gottschalk)

9 – "There's a Mate in This Big World for You" – OZMA (Morosco/Schertzinger)

10 – "Ask the Flowers to Tell You" – OZMA and FILES (Baum/Gottschalk)

11 – "Dear Old Hank" – BETSY (Baum/Gottschalk)

12 – "Act One Finale" – PRINCIPALS and FIELD FLOWERS (Baum/Gottschalk)

13 – Entr'acte – The Tik-Tok Man of Oz "Lanciers" (Gottschalk)

MUSICAL NUMBERS

ACT TWO

14 – "Work, Lads, Work" – RUGGEDO with METAL IMPS (Baum/Gottschalk)

15 – "When in Trouble Come to Papa" – RUGGEDO and POLYCHROME (Baum/Gottschalk)

16 – "Fight for Oogaboo" - ANN and ARMY OF OOGABOO (Baum/Gottschalk)

17 – "Imps March" – Dance of METAL IMPS (Gottschalk)

18 - "Rainbow Bride" – POLYCHROME with RUGGEDO, ANN, SHAGGY, BETSY, and TIK-TOK (Baum/Gottschalk)

19 – "My Wonderful Dream Girl" – FILES (Morosco/Schertzinger)

20 – "Folly!" – TIK-TOK, BETSY, and SHAGGY (Baum/Gottschalk)

21 – "Oh! Take Me" – OZMA and FILES (Morosco/Schertzinger)

22 - "Just for Fun" – OZMA and FILES (Baum/Gottschalk)

23 – Dance of the Rainbows from "Oh! My Bow" (Gottschalk)

23-B – "Forgotten" (Optional) – RUGGEDO
Lyrics by Flora Wulschner, music by Eugene Cowles

24 – "So Do I!" – TIK-TOK and RUGGEDO (Baum/Gottschalk)

24-B - "One! Two! Three! All Over" (Optional) - SHAGGY, RUGGEDO, and TIK-TOK
Lyrics by Paul West, music by Safford Waters

25 – "The Waltz Scream" – ANN and SHAGGY (Baum/Gottschalk)

26 – "The Magnet of Love" Reprise (Chorus) – ALL (Baum/Gottschalk)

The Tik-Tok Man of Oz Piano-Vocal Score (ISBN 978-1-929527-30-4) is available separately.

Characters from the original production of The Tik-Tok Man of Oz, *top, left to right: Betsy Bobbin and Hank the Mule, Tik-Tok and the Shaggy Man, Ruggedo the Metal Monarch; bottom, left to right: Private Files and Polychrome the Rainbow's Daughter, the Buttercup Chorus.*

NOTES ON STAGING THE TIK-TOK MAN OF OZ

THE ORIGINAL 1913–14 production of *The Tik-Tok Man of Oz* was an elaborate musical extravaganza, intended to be a sumptuous visual spectacle, filled with dozens of chorus members both female and male, special effects, and lavish scenery. But a new production can be effective without being so elaborate. The script in this volume is intended to be adaptable to nearly any scale of production.

CAST SIZE

A cast of nine principal roles and a chorus of twelve members makes the smallest effective cast size TWENTY-ONE in number. A cast size of sixteen, including a small chorus of seven members also performing all the minor roles, might possibly work. But the confrontation between the Army of Oogaboo and the Metal Imps in Act Two might lose a lot of effectiveness with so few chorus members.

The cast can easily expand to accommodate many more than the minimum required. Schools and studios desiring to cast a great many students might cast each chorus group separately, i. e. the Waves, Metal Imps, Army of Oogaboo, Field Flowers, Rainbow Girls, etc., so that no chorus member plays more than one role. This provides the greatest number of opportunities to participate. Large choruses will increase the effectiveness of all scenes involving a chorus.

SCENES

PRELUDE – A STORM AT SEA

A ship sinking on a stormy sea, with Betsy and Hank clinging to wreckage, might be presented in many different ways. The original production featured the actors on a realistic hencoop, or raft, among physical scenery: ground rows painted as waves, a seascape back drop, a miniature ship, and a projected water effect.

The 2014 revival utilized more modern, kabuki-like techniques, featuring several long swaths of blue China silk pre-set flat on the stage floor. A stage hand or chorus member, dressed in black, slowly carried an ocean liner cut-out across the stage during the last part of the overture. As the storm at sea ensued, chorus members billowed the China silk rhythmically up and down to evoke ocean waves. They started calmly, then became more agitated as the storm progressed. The ship was eventually overwhelmed by the waves and disappeared. Chorus members, representing the waves, swung around a small child dressed the same as the adult actor playing Betsy, as well as a large toy mule representing Hank.

This scene might be presented as a dance number. A large chorus of actors or dancers playing waves could effectively mimic a sea both calm and stormy. The waves might carry a model of Betsy's ship and overwhelm it, then pass around models of Betsy and Hank with a raft or piece of floating wreckage. Alternatively, the actors playing Betsy and Hank might body surf, as in a mosh pit, if enough actors are playing waves to support them.

ACT ONE
SCENE ONE – THE ROSE KINGDOM

The original production featured a detailed set representing a glass-walled conservatory filled with rose bushes. Chorus members wore headdresses to represent rose blossoms. They bent their heads down, so that the headdresses concealed their faces, then raised their heads all in a single moment to reveal their faces, creating a striking visual effect. A scrim hid the upstage area where the Royal Rose Bush stood. At the proper moment, lights behind the scrim went on, making the scrim transparent, to reveal the Royal Rose Bush to the audience. A huge, mechanical rose opened, revealing Ozma the Rose Princess growing on the Royal Rose Bush.

In the 2014 revival, flats with large painted roses on both sides of the stage represented the Rose Kingdom. Actors in the roles of Moss Rose and Jacque Rose stood on 18-inch square black boxes. To represent the Royal Rose Bush, chorus members entered holding a large green blanket like a curtain. The blanket, decorated with leaf patterns, concealed Ozma the Rose Princess. At the proper moment, the chorus members turned the blanket around to reveal Ozma.

The important aspect of the scene is to create a sense of many roses growing in a tended garden. Techniques such as painted roses on scenery, prop roses set around the stage, chorus members dressed as roses, and rose-colored lights might be used singly or in combination for this scene.

SCENE TWO – CROSSROADS WITH A WELL

The original production featured a backdrop painted to represent a vast field of wildflowers stretching into the distance. Polychrome descended from the fly-space above, lowered to the stage on two wires. Tik-Tok appeared from a large square well with a roof and a working windlass with a hook.

These ideas can be greatly simplified, if desired. In the 2014 production, Polychrome and her sisters danced onto the stage from the wings, while lighting represented the rainbow. Different colored lights set all the way upstage filled the entire backdrop with vertical stripes of light in rainbow colors. These were controlled from the lighting board and created an effective rainbow at the proper moments in the show. A projected rainbow might work as well. Alternatively, a large fabric backdrop similar to a rainbow flag—or long strips of fabric in rainbow colors—might be hung from the flies and raised and lowered as needed.

In the 2014 production, chorus members dressed in black carried on a three-sided prop well that concealed the actor playing Tik-Tok. Compartments inside the well contained various props that the Shaggy Man pulled from the well. At the proper moment, chorus members revolved the well until the open fourth side revealed Tik-Tok sitting on the stage. The other principal actors pulled Tik-Tok to a standing position.

Scene Three - Field of Flowers

Wildflowers must be prominently represented in this scene, Like the Roses in Scene One, flowers can be painted on scenery or set onstage as props, or the chorus can be dressed as flowers.

In the 1913 production, a backdrop presented flower fields stretching far into the distance, while chorus members portrayed Daisies, Buttercups, and Wild Roses during "Ask the Flowers to Tell You."

For that number in the 2014 revival, Private Files carried a large daisy prop, while dancers representing dream versions of Files and Ozma performed a ballet. Chorus members must also fill Field Flower roles for the "Act One Finale."

Act Two
Scene One – The Metal Monarch's Underground Cavern

In the original production, scenery representing stalactites and stalagmites filled the stage. Among the scenery stood anvils on several levels. The Metal Monarch's large throne sat at center stage. During the "Work, Lads, Work" musical number, the chorus of Metal Imps struck the anvils with hammers in time to the music.

In the 2014 revival, the anvils of the Metal Imps were represented by two 18-inch square black boxes, which the chorus struck with silver mallets in time to the music. Lighting effects were used to indicate the moments when Ruggedo accidentally lights the furnaces and when the tin mine caves in.

Scene Two - Caves and Chasm

Depending on how elaborate a production is planned, the scenery can be changed to a representation of tunnels or caverns in another part of the Metal Monarch's underground domain. An indication of a canyon-like chasm should be included. If the scenery appears naturalistic, a visible opening to the sky should also be incorporated, so that the rainbow's appearance makes sense.

In the 2014 production, the Metal Monarch had no throne, so no scenery changed when the characters left the throne room of Scene One.

Elaborate scenery might be built to represent the chasm that the principal characters cross on the rainbow, but the front edge of the stage might serve as the chasm, and the rainbow effect can be achieved with colored lights.

Scene Three – The Metal Forest

Indications of trees formed from silver and gold metal are necessary to this scene. Metal bushes, vines, and any other metal vegetation can be added as desired. Trees and vegetation might be set with colored plastic gems. For the 2014 revival, flats with 2-dimensional representations of silver trees stood at both sides of the stage. They were embellished with silver leaves and small mirror-balls representing fruit. Chorus members held 3-dimensional silver branches at various positions around the stage.

Principal Characters and Costumes

BETSY BOBBIN, a girl from Oklahoma, is probably anywhere from twelve to sixteen years old. Betsy's costume might look like clothes from any time beginning in the early twentieth century up to the present, as long as the costume doesn't suggest a character too mature. Betsy is young, earnest, and open to adventure.

HANK THE MULE is a special type of role, similar to the role of Nana the nursemaid dog in *Peter Pan* or to the role of Milky White the cow in *Into the Woods* when that part is played by an actor. In the original production, Hank was played by an actor that specialized in impersonating animals. He performed Hank bent over, holding onto arm extensions ending in hooves, and played a fairly realistic mule.

Today, professional animal impersonators are few and far between. In the 2014 revival, Hank was presented more like a sports team mascot, occasionally on all fours, but frequently standing upright. Hank's role might be filled by an acrobat who can perform stunts to amaze the audience. Above all, Hank should be funny. The script specifies opportunities for Hank to chase other characters, interact with objects from the well, etc. Take full advantage of these opportunities and give Hank plenty of humorous antics. Add more as seems appropriate. Hank should be especially fond and protective of Betsy.

A costume for Hank the Mule could range from a realistic-looking mule suit, completely concealing the actor, to something much simpler, such as a gray sweatshirt, gray sweatpants, black sneakers, and gray mule ears fixed to the actor's head.

In the original production of *The Tik-Tok Man of Oz*, Hank proved to be one of the popular features of the show.

No reason exists that Hank can't be just as popular in any new production.

THE SHAGGY MAN is an easy-going, jolly wanderer who loves to eat apples. His age isn't particularly important. His costume might be from any period, but it must have shags. Whether the shags are simply rips in the costume or lengths of fabric applied to the costume or some other means to make the actor appear shaggy, the shags must be clearly visible to the back row of the audience. Shaggy carries the Love Magnet, which must also be large enough for the entire audience to see.

OZMA THE ROSE PRINCESS is an elegant young woman in both personality and appearance. Her costume should present some suggestion of roses, if only red or pink in color. In 2014, Ozma wore a large rose on top of her head and a red sequined gown slit up the side and with a low neckline to emphasize her sex appeal.

POLYCHROME THE RAINBOW'S DAUGHTER is a sprightly young woman, preferably a dancer. Her costume should suggest the rainbow. Vertically striped rainbow fabric is a good choice. Sparkles on her costume or as part of her make-up can add a pleasing effect. If the actor wears her hair long, a headband or ribbon should be used to keep her hair from whipping her face while she dances.

TIK-TOK is a copper man who runs by clockwork. His costume should be completely copper-colored. Gears and bits that light up might be added, anything that might emphasize his mechanical nature. In both the original production and in the 2014 revival, the actor playing Tik-Tok wore a circular chestplate that represented a window revealing the wheels and gears of Tik-Tok's inner workings.

Tik-Tok's costume must have three key-holes to wind up Tik-Tok—one under the left arm, one under the right arm, and one in the center of the chest. The key to wind Tik-Tok should be fixed to the costume in such a way that it can be removed and replaced. The 2104 production accomplished this by incorporating small, strong magnets into the prop key and into the back of the costume just below the neck, so that the key stuck firmly to Tik-Tok. Magnets were also incorporated into the keyholes on the costume to facilitate the effect of winding. Tik-Tok should have fixed to his back in some manner a sign with his guarantee and directions for use. In the final scene, a trap door large enough for the Love Magnet must open and close somewhere on Tik-Tok's costume, preferably on chest or head.

The actor playing Tik-Tok should move mechanically. The actor should speak mechanically, too, but not in such a monotonous tone as to become irritating to the audience. Particular attention must be paid to Tik-Tok's three stages of being wound up, so that, for instance, the actor doesn't move when Tik-Tok's movement is wound down.

The roles of Tik-Tok and the Shaggy Man were originally conceived for a comedy team. The traditional comedy team that evolved from vaudeville is old-fashioned now, but descendants of the tradition can still be seen in movies starring Laurel and Hardy, Abbott and Costello, and to some extent the Three Stooges and the Marx Brothers. Tik-Tok and Shaggy should take every opportunity to display plenty of funny interaction and physical comedy with each other. Even when one antagonizes the other for the sake of amusement, at heart their friendship remains loyal.

QUEEN ANN SOFORTH, demanding and imperious, is more than just the leader of the Army of Oogaboo, she is also royalty. Both these facts give her an inflated sense of importance. Her costume should indicate both her military and royal statuses, and could well be exaggerated in flashiness and pomposity to reflect her proud personality.

PRIVATE FILES is young, trim, and should look dashing in his army uniform. He's well-meaning, but he's probably a little too handsome and a little too stupid for his own good—lots of style, but not a lot of substance. He holds the rank of private, so his uniform shouldn't be too fancy, though it should appear unique and striking.

The romance between Private Files and Ozma should contain a hint of sexuality, as long as it avoids vulgarity.

RUGGEDO THE METAL MONARCH appears imposing and grand. He is not evil, so much as childish in his attempts to gain his desires. His costume should feature metal and metallic colors, likely silver and gold. Metallic make-up covering the actor's exposed skin might be a good touch. Ruggedo wears the Magic Belt, which has buttons that he can punch with his fingers to work magic. The shape, color, and style of belt and buttons are open to the designer's imagination.

"The Clockwork Man" Musical Number

In the original production of *The Tik-Tok Man of Oz*, a Clock Girl chorus of women wearing cuckoo clock-like headdresses, with their faces showing instead of clock faces, joined Tik-Tok for "The Clockwork Man" musical number. If desired, a similar chorus of Clock Girls might be added to "The Clockwork Man" number to sing the "tik, tok" lyrics in place of (or along with) Betsy and Shaggy. The chorus might be dressed as clocks or gears or they might swing pendulums.

An idea for the 2014 production featured chorus members, wearing black shirts decorated with copper-colored gears, that joined Tik-Tok in this number, but these Clock Girls were cut during rehearsal.

NOTES ON STAGING

THE ARMY OF OOGABOO

Queen Ann's army is intended to include sixteen officers and a single private. The officers' names are: General Fuss, General De Bility, General Ization, General Shipp, Colonel Korn, Colonel Nutt, Colonel Wheete, Colonel Shuck, Major Key, Major Ity, Major Doughmeaux, Major Niener, Captain Young, Captain Phresh, Captain Crewd, and Captain Strutt.

More officers may be added, as desired. Fewer officers will do, as well, though during the musical number "The Army of Oogaboo," Private Files might join in singing the officers' parts as well as his own if too few officers can't effectively carry the song.

Private Files, as a principal role, should be visually distinguishable from the rest of the army. This might simply be accomplished by a giving Private Files a different color uniform than the rest of the army. Or the officers might be more elaborately costumed, plumes on their helmets, gold sashes, lots of medals, etc.—visually very busy—while Private Files wears a plain and simple but visually stronger uniform, so that he stands out from the crowd.

If the officers of the Army of Oogaboo carry or wear swords or guns, the actors should be drilled not to bump their weapons into each other—unless purposely staged for comic effect. Any weapons should be mainly decorative, since the officers don't expect to fight.

"IMPS MARCH" MUSICAL NUMBER

In Act Two, the chorus of Metal Imps performs a precision march to a musical number. This is intended as a spectacular visual feature and should be choreographed to give the impression that the Metal Monarch commands such powerful forces, that the Army of Oogaboo is foolish to challenge it. The number might also be staged as a battle between the Metal Imps and the Army of Oogaboo, with the Army of Oogaboo being completely overwhelmed by the end.

In case a small chorus can't pull this off effectively, the "Imps March" might be moved to the opening number of Act Two, as a dance rather than a precision march, and segue directly into the musical number "Work, Lads, Work." That is how the 2014 production staged the "Imps March."

THE RECONSTRUCTION OF TIK-TOK

The reconstruction of Tik-Tok in Act Two is an ancient bit of stage magic. All portions of the actor playing Tik-Tok should be first wrapped in pieces of black fabric. Then the actor should stand in front of a black curtain, so that from the audience, the black-wrapped figure appears invisible within a black space. Keep the lighting of this effect dim and avoid lighting any black fabric directly. Vertical slits have been previously cut into the black curtain. As each prop piece of the exploded

Tik-Tok is set into place against the black fabric, it is passed through a slit and the black wrapping, which conceals the corresponding body part of the actor playing Tik-Tok, should be removed. The actor playing Ruggedo, the Metal Monarch, should position his own body to block as much of this activity from the audience as possible, stepping aside at intervals to reveal that Tik-Tok is gradually being restored, until Tik-Tok stands whole again.

The black curtain should be hung within a black or very dark area of the stage. It might be rigged between two metal trees. Or the black fabric might be made to look as if it's actually a cave opening or tunnel entrance leading from the underground cavern of the Metal Forest.

Be careful if using velcro to fasten the pieces of fabric concealing Tik-Tok. If the audience can detect the sound of velcro ripping apart, the illusion may be destroyed.

However, Tik-Tok's reconstruction needn't be so elaborate. In the 2014 production, to show that Tik-Tok had been damaged, dislodged gears hung on wires from Tik-Tok's mechanical chestplate and the battery-operated electric light that illuminated Tik-Tok's chestplate from within was turned off. To restore Tik-Tok, Ruggedo pushed the gears back into position on the chestplate while surreptitiously turning on the light.

THE UGLY MAN

In the final scene, the Ugly Man is dressed in old tatters. His face must remain completely hidden from the audience until he is disenchanted. When the Ugly Man moves his mask slightly aside for the females to kiss him and for Ruggedo to examine him, the actor should face sideways and shift the handkerchief on his upstage side. Casting a good-looking actor in the role of the Ugly Man will give his disenchantment the most impact.

The roles of the Hank the Mule, the Royal Gardener, and the Messenger of the Rose Kingdom can be filled by actors of either gender. The Gardener and the Messenger may be combined and played by a single actor.

KEEPS ON TICKING

The foregoing notes are intended as springboards to start your production team on its own path toward solutions to mounting *The Tik-Tok Man of Oz*. With a bit of thought and planning, the direction, designing, and staging of *The Tik-Tok Man of Oz* can fit the cast size and budget available to your group.

For a resource beyond these notes, consult the companion volume to this script, *All Wound Up: The Making of The Tik-Tok Man of Oz*, which contains a wealth of images and insights from both the original production and the 2014 revival of the show.

THE TIK-TOK MAN OF OZ

Musical Number 1 – Overture – The Tik-Tok Man of Oz "Selection"

PRELUDE

Musical Number 2 – "A Storm at Sea"

(A ship on the horizon founders and breaks up. Dancers representing storm-tossed WAVES dance across stage, carrying a model of a chicken coop with a girl and a mule clinging to it.)

ACT ONE

SCENE ONE – The Rose Kingdom. The stage is set to represent a glass-walled conservatory full of rose bushes. In foreground are actors dressed as ROSES, grouped with bowed heads so their faces are not seen.

(ENTER BETSY BOBBIN, followed by HANK, her mule. BETSY peers curiously around and disturbs MOSS ROSE, who haughtily raises head and looks at BETSY. HANK has business sniffing at roses, particularly at JACQUE ROSE.)

MOSS ROSE:

What an impolite intrusion!

HANK:

Hee-haw!

BETSY:

Couldn't help it, folks. I've just been wrecked.

ROSES: *(Raising faces)*

Wrecked!

BETSY:

Cor-rect. Ship went down—I stayed up.

JACQUE ROSE:

This is a private greenhouse, devoted to the culture of the rarest and fairest roses ever grown. You must leave us at once!

BETSY: *(To mule)*

Did you hear that, Hank! We stranded on the strand outside and rushed in here for a welcome. And now—now—they want to turn us out, and we've no place to go! You'll comfort me, won't you, dear old Hank?

(HANK tries to embrace her and pat her head.)

HANK:

Hee-haw!

ROSES: *(Shrinking back)*

Oh—h—h!

MOSS ROSE:

This is our own special hot-house. Only roses are allowed here.

BETSY:

Don't you need a gardener?

JACQUE ROSE:

We have one who is responsible for our culture and beauty.

(ENTER royal GARDENER, hastily.)

GARDENER:

Here I am!

ACT ONE, SCENE ONE

(HANK falls back on haunches in surprise, then chases GARDENER, who Exits.)

(Crash of glass is heard. Enter SHAGGY MAN, falling onto stage—from above, if possible. BETSY and HANK approach SHAGGY and examine him curiously. He is eating an apple, which he continues to munch, paying no attention to his surroundings.)

BETSY:

Good gracious! Where did you come from?

SHAGGY MAN:

From outside. I climbed an apple tree over yonder, and the branch gave way. I took a drop too much and here I am. *(Looks around for the first time.)* I see I've broken into good society.

BETSY:

Yes, you're in good company. Lots of these roses are porch-climbers. Say, gimme an apple.

SHAGGY:

Apples aren't good for little girls. They've caused most of the trouble in this world, from Eve down.

Musical Number 3 – "An Apple's the Cause of It All" – SHAGGY MAN

SHAGGY MAN:

In historee an apple tree
In the Garden of Eden stood,
And Adam and Eve did both believe
Its fruit was not much good.
Then 'long came a serpent, mighty slick,
And told 'em an apple they should pick
And eat it quick, and they did the trick,
And the apple made 'em sick!

And so you see, in historee
An apple's the cause of the fall;
To eat it was surely considered unlawful,
But Eve took a bite and Adam a jawful;
The pain that it gave 'em was just something awful!
An apple's the cause of it all!

An apple makes more tummy aches
Than rarebits, lobsters, cheese;
The doctor comes, looks wise, haw-hums,
And tries your pain to ease.
But the apple laughs at the doctor's pill
And the sexton digs in the graveyard still,
If the wicked apple has its will,
It always fights to kill.

And so I eat 'em sour or sweet,
And wish I could eat 'em all;
It's a matter of tastes and the more diabolic
Your agony is, why, the more it will frolic.
And if you expire in a fit of the colic,
An apple's the cause of it all!

BETSY:

This hothouse is devoted 'specially to roses. They've turned me out, and I
'spect they'll turn you out too.

SHAGGY:

Nothing ever turns out the way you expect. *(Points to mule.)* Who's your
friend?

BETSY:

His name's Hank. Isn't it a pretty name? I'm Betsy. What's your name?

ACT ONE, SCENE ONE

SHAGGY:

They call me Shaggy Man. Lost the family bible and can't remember what I was christened. Very young at the time.

BETSY:

How did you happen to stray into these gardens?

SHAGGY:

Looking for brother. Brother and I owned a mine in Colorado. Scooped out gold nuggets by the pail-full. Oh, joy! One day I left brother digging in the mine. When I came back he was gone—the mine was gone—everything gone. Oh, gloom!

BETSY:

How strange!

SHAGGY:

Couldn't understand it at first. Then I found, on the spot where the mine had been, an asbestos letter. Here it is. *(Hands piece of asbestos to BETSY.)*

BETSY: *(Reads)*

"This mine is mine so I've taken it away to my underground kingdom and with it the audacious mortal who was robbing me of my gold. Let this be a warning to mankind not to interfere with the rights of, Signed, Ruggedo, the Metal Monarch." Goodness, me! Who's this Metal Monarch?

SHAGGY:

A hard question. He's metal.

BETSY:

I've heard of the copper king, and the steel king, but I never before heard of the Metal Monarch. Where does he live?

ACT ONE, SCENE ONE

SHAGGY:

He didn't give his address.

BETSY:

Is your brother still in his power?

SHAGGY:

Sure thing. Brother's broke out of jail seven times, but the Metal Kingdom must be too strong for him. Never mind. I'll find brother some day.

BETSY:

How?

SHAGGY:

Can't imagine. But as long as I've got the Love Magnet I'm not worrying.

BETSY:

What is the Love Magnet?

SHAGGY: (Mysteriously, seizing her wrist)

Sh—h—h! New invention: Dan Cupid, patentee. Whoever owns the Love Magnet wins the love of everyone he meets. No courting, car-fare, flowers or theatre tickets. No trouble to borrow money, always welcome when you visit friends. Fine, ain't it? I own this Love Magnet, and—here it is!

(SHAGGY takes from his pocket a shining silver magnet. BETSY leans against SHAGGY and put her arms around his neck. HANK comes and kneels at his feet and rubs his head against SHAGGY's legs.)

(ENTER GARDENER.)

GARDENER:

Say, folks, you've no right here.

ACT ONE, SCENE ONE

(GARDENER sees Love Magnet and immediately tries to embrace SHAGGY.)

GARDENER:
Say! You're the best thing that ever happened, even if you are shaggy.

(HANK chases GARDENER off stage. Both Exit.)

SHAGGY: *(To BETSY)*
You see, my dear, the Magnet works perfectly.

BETSY:

Gee! I wish I had it!

(BETSY takes Love Magnet from SHAGGY.)

MUSICAL NUMBER 4 – "THE MAGNET OF LOVE" – BETSY

BETSY:
When you feel a funny feeling
That you never felt before;
When a yearn is o'er you stealing
For the maiden you adore,
There's a pow'r that sets your glowing heart a flutter,
Puts the love-light in your eyes:
There's a necromancy causes you to utter
Tender rhapsodies and plaintive sighs.
So beware! Have a care!

'Tis the wonderful Magnet of Love,
It's a charm from the fairies above,
So you can't get away from its magical sway,
It holds you a captive, object as you may.
It is folly its pow'r to resist

When it gives all your heart strings a twist
For you'll "bill" and you'll "coo," like a daft turtle dove,
'Neath the charm of the Magnet of Love.

When a boy and girl go crazy
Singing to a cold, hard moon;
When their intellects are hazy,
Namby pamby love-lays croon;
When a homely girl is loved by an Apollo,
Who for her grim smiles will sigh,
When a rosy peach some ugly chap will follow
And you can't explain the reason why:
Here's the fact; quite exact:

'Tis the wonderful Magnet of Love,
It's a charm from the fairies above,
So you can't get away from its magical sway,
It holds you a captive, object as you may;
It is folly its pow'r to resist
When it gives all your heart strings a twist
For you'll "bill" and you'll "coo," like a daft turtle dove,
'Neath the charm of the Magnet of Love.

(SHAGGY takes the Love Magnet back from BETSY.)

SHAGGY:

There's only this one in the world, and I intend to hang on to it.

(ENTER GARDENER, chased by HANK.)

GARDENER:

I, myself, love you dearly—

ACT ONE, SCENE ONE

HANK:

Hee-haw!

GARDENER:

But you are intruding and it's my duty to arrest you.

SHAGGY:

Arrest us!

BETSY:

Law's sake. Who makes the rules and regulations of this place?

GARDENER:

Not me. They're printed in a book. *(Takes book from pocket and reads)* Page 13. If any strangers enter, they must be arrested and put to death, being condemned by the ruler.

SHAGGY:

I haven't been condemned by a ruler since I was a school boy. Where is he? Trot out your ruler.

GARDENER:

There isn't one just now. You see, the rulers of the Rose Kingdom all grow on bushes in the Royal Gardens. Last one we had got buggy, so we had to plant him before his time. Just now there's none ripe enough to pick.

BETSY:

Where are the Royal Gardens?

ROSES and GARDENER:

Here!

ACT ONE, SCENE ONE

(The Royal Gardens appear. On a low limb is OZMA, the Rose Princess. She stands motionless, but is evidently all ready to pick.)

BETSY: *(Approaching bush, admiring OZMA)*
Oh, isn't she lovely! Let's pick her for a ruler.

GARDENER:
No! This *(pointing to OZMA)* is a Royal Princess, and her name is Ozma. But the subjects of the Rose Kingdom don't want a girl ruler—they want a man. A King, see?

BETSY:
Let's pick her, Shaggy.

SHAGGY:
All right.

(HANK chases GARDENER off stage. EXIT GARDENER, while HANK remains on stage to stand guard. BETSY and SHAGGY lift OZMA from the limb to the ground where she first exhibits life, smiling on BETSY and SHAGGY and making a courtesy by way of thanks. The ROSES turn, murmuring with indignation.)

MOSS ROSE:
Audacious mortal! What have you done?

BETSY:
Picked a princess for you; that's all.

JACQUE ROSE:
No girl shall rule us!

OZMA:
Have I no welcome, pretty subjects? Have I not come from my royal tree to be your princess?

24

ACT ONE, SCENE ONE

ROSES:

No, no!

MOSS ROSE:

Turn her out with the others.

BETSY: *(Pleadingly)*

Don't turn us away—please don't! We've no place to go.

OZMA:

Dare you exile me—a Royal Princess—from my own Kingdom?

JACQUE ROSE:

We dare, and we will.

ROSES:

Go!

(ROSES point to exit. BETSY, HANK, OZMA with bowed head, and SHAGGY Exit, urged on by ROSES, who follow them off stage. End of Scene One.)

SCENE TWO – A Cross Roads, with a well.

Musical Number 5 – "Oh! My Bow" – POLYCHROME

(Dance Music from "Oh! My Bow" begins. The rainbow appears, with POLY-CHROME, the Rainbow's Daughter, dancing, accompanied by RAINBOW GIRLS. Rainbow fades and RAINBOW GIRLS Exit. POLYCHROME, turning, sees the rainbow disappear and in despair extends her arms toward it.)

POLYCHROME:

Oh, oh! There goes the rainbow—and my sisters with it! Dear me! What shall I do? How careless of me to step foot on this cold earth. And here I must stay—an outcast from the sky—until the rainbow comes again.

ACT ONE, SCENE TWO

POLYCHROME:
Ev'ry maiden ought to have, (so I've understood)
Just one bow to comfort her, yes, she really should;
But, alas! it's come to pass, I'm deserted quite;
Not a bow have I in tow, oh, what a sorry plight!

I'm forlorn and dreary, I have lost my bow!
There is none to cheer me, I've no place to go.
Any bow is charming, maidens all agree;
None is quite alarming, oh! dear me!

There are many kinds of beaux, beaming bright and gay,
And the right one, I suppose, never came my way;
But the bow I love the best, rainbow in the sky,
Now has left me and bereft me, as I vainly sigh:

I'm forlorn and dreary, I have lost my bow!
There is none to cheer me, I've no place to go.
Beaux are to a maiden a necess-i-tee,
I'm with sorrow laden, oh! dear me!

*(ENTER BETSY, HANK, OZMA, and SHAGGY MAN. HANK goes to the well
and examines it.)*

BETSY: *(Running to POLYCHROME)*
Oh, what a darling creature!

POLYCHROME:
Who are you?

SHAGGY:
We're wanderers. Welcome to our hospitality, little Rainbow. *(Bows to
her.)*

ACT ONE, SCENE TWO

POLYCHROME:

I'm called Polychrome.

BETSY:

Polly-chrome! Sounds like a cross between a parrot and a paint box. May I call you Polly?

POLYCHROME: *(Sobbing)*

If you like. I'm the most miserable girl in the whole world. I've lost my bow!

SHAGGY:

Take me!

POLYCHROME: *(Stamping her foot)*

I don't want you! I want my rain-bow!

SHAGGY:

Don't I reign in your heart?

Musical Number 6 – "I Want to Be Somebody's Girlie" – POLYCHROME

POLYCHROME:

For a girlie of my size,
I have not grown very wise
As to what a girl should do when she's in love;
Though I've always had my beaux,
There are many things, you know,
They do diff'rent when you're someone's turtle dove;
Take for instance how a fellow
Looks for hours in the eyes
Of some pretty little girlie,
Then he sighs and sighs and sighs,

Swears he never loved another,
Tells a lot of pretty lies,
And he knows he can't afford
To pay for half the things he buys;
Oh! it's all in the game, I guess,
And I really, really might as well confess:

I want to be somebody's girlie,
I want to be somebody's Pearlie,
I want to feel two arms around me,
Arms that are really glad they've found me;
I want someone to hug and kiss me,
When I'm away some one to miss me,
Of ev'ry thing grand in this wide, wide world
I want to be somebody's girl.

I want to be somebody's girlie,
I want to be somebody's Pearlie,
I want to feel two arms around me,
Arms that are really glad they've found me;
I want someone to hug and kiss me,
When I'm away some one to miss me,
Of ev'ry thing grand in this wide, wide world
I want to be somebody's girl.

SHAGGY:

Never mind; you may join our party until you find your bow again.

POLYCHROME:

I don't like you.

SHAGGY:

No? *(Holds up Love Magnet.)*

ACT ONE, SCENE TWO

POLYCHROME:

(Clasps her hands ecstatically and advances eagerly toward SHAGGY)
I—love—you!

SHAGGY:

Of course; but you can't help it, so it's no credit to you.

VOICE: *(of TIK-TOK in well)*

Hel-lup! Hel-lup! Hel-lup!

(All start—HANK falls back on his haunches, wagging his ears.)

BETSY:

What was that?

OZMA:

Didn't someone cry for help?

VOICE:

Oh, hel-lup! Oh, hel-lup! Oh, hel—g-r-r-r-r-----

SHAGGY: *(Goes to well)*

Look here, Betsy! I believe old Hank was hankering for something strange in this well. *(Together BETSY and SHAGGY look down well.)* Let's see what it is. *(SHAGGY winds up chain and dumps old hoop-skirt on stage. Then comes a dead cat.)* Ding-dong-dell—pussy in the well. *(Next he brings up small toy mule.)* Why, Hank, here's your brother. *(Throws toy to HANK who has business with it.)* Hello! There's something more down here, I guess. *(Drops bucket again.)*

BETSY:

Up with it, then.

(SHAGGY draws up bucket with difficulty and dumps on stage TIK-TOK who is huddled in a heap and lies motionless. BETSY and SHAGGY look at him curiously, while HANK prances around in joy.)

BETSY:

Looks like a copper man. Here's a sign on his back. *(She kneels beside TIK-TOK and reads.)* Smith and Tinker's patent adjustable, triple-action, automatic Clockwork Man, Tik-Tok. Mechanism guaranteed for a thousand years. Any infringement will be promptly prosecuted.

OZMA:

Dear me!

POLYCHROME:

How strange!

SHAGGY:

He's a wonder!

BETSY:

But here's more. *(Reads)* "Directions for use—wind up the clockwork man under the left arm and he will thinks as cleverly as a trained rooster— wind under his right arm and he will speak like a small black demitasse orator—wind him under his wishbone and he will move in a natural and intelligent manner and act as cleverly as Henry Irving." *(To others)* He ought to work, if we wind him up.

POLYCHROME:

Where's the key?

SHAGGY:

(Picking up key from where it hangs at the top of TIK-TOK's back or from where it has fallen onto the floor) This must be it.

(BETSY and SHAGGY raise TIK-TOK to his feet and move his joints so that he will stand up. He sways and topples until they get him balanced.)

BETSY: *(Waves key)*

What part of him shall I wind up first?

OZMA:

His thoughts of course.

BETSY:

Which is his left arm?

POLYCHROME: *(Pointing)*

That's the right one.

BETSY:

But I want the left.

SHAGGY:

Of course. The left one's the right one, isn't it?

(BETSY winds TIK-TOK under left arm.)

OZMA:

Listen! Can't you hear him tick!

(All gather close and listen.)

SHAGGY:

Wind up his phonograph, Betsy, and see if that ticks.

BETSY: *(Flourishing key)*

Which is the right arm?

ACT ONE, SCENE TWO

POLYCHROME:

The one left.

(BETSY winds TIK-TOK under right arm.)

TIK-TOK: *(Always speaks in monotone.)*

Ma-ny thanks.

(All start back, surprised.)

SHAGGY:

Well, his Victrola's all right, but I'm inclined to doubt his think-works.

TIK-TOK:

When in doubt, breed mumps—

BETSY:

You mean, lead trumps.

TIK-TOK:

I mean what I say.

SHAGGY:

You're wrong.

TIK-TOK:

I'm right ac-cor-ding to my ma-chin-er-y.

SHAGGY:

Then your machinery is out of gear.

TIK-TOK:

Don't blame me, blame the—z-z-z—pa-ten-tee. Wind me tight and I'll show you, I'm all right and can go.

ACT ONE, SCENE TWO

BETSY:

Here we go. I may be encouraging another bad actor; but that's not my fault.

(Follow directions in the score to align the following actions with the music: BETSY winds TIK-TOK on breast in time to music. — TIK-TOK moves. — He stops. — BETSY winds again in jerks. — TIK-TOK moves again. — TIK-TOK shows life. — BETSY overjoyed. — TIK-TOK takes a step.)

MUSICAL NUMBER 7 – "THE CLOCKWORK MAN" – TIK-TOK with CHORUS

TIK-TOK and (CHORUS):
I'm a man of many parts and complicated
Clockwork makes me go; (Tik-Tok)
I can run because I'm finely regulated,
Never fast or slow: (Tik-Tok)
Right on time you're always sure to find me; (Tik-Tok, Tik-Tok)
If my works run down you mustn't mind me, (Tik-Tok, Tik-Tok)
Take the key and then proceed to wind me
And my genius I will show. (Tik-Tok)

Always work and never play! (Tik-Tok, Tik-Tok)
Don't demand a cent of pay! (Tik-Tok, Tik-Tok)
What I'm wound to do I do do, (Tik-Tok, Tik-Tok)
Isn't that the nicest way? (Tik-Tok, Tik-Tok)
I'm a very clever man! (Tik-Tok, Tik-Tok)
Find my equal if you can! (Tik-Tok, Tik-Tok)
When you wind me you will find me (Tik-Tok, Tik-Tok)
Working on the clockwork plan! (Tik-Tok, Tik-Tok)

(TIK-TOK) and CHORUS:
Always work and never play! (Tik)
Don't demand a cent of pay! (Tok)

What he's wound to do he'll do, too,
Isn't that the nicest way? (Tik-Tok)
He's a very clever man! (Tik)
Find his equal if you can, (Tok)
When you wind him you will find him
Working on the clockwork plan, Tik-Tok.

TIK-TOK and (CHORUS):
Mortal man has no stem-winding works to guide him
When he gets too fast. (Tik-Tok)
No one knows what deviltry there lurks inside him
Till the action's past. (Tik-Tok)
In my case I'm always true and trusty; (Tik-Tok, Tik-Tok)
Never get too musty or too dusty; (Tik-Tok, Tik-Tok)
Keep me oiled and I am never rusty
And a thousand years I'll last (Tik-Tok)

(TIK-TOK) and CHORUS:
Always work and never play! (Tik)
Don't demand a cent of pay! (Tok)
What he's wound to do he'll do, too,
Isn't that the nicest way? (Tik-Tok)
He's a very clever man! (Tik)
Find his equal if you can, (Tok)
When you wind him you will find him

TIK-TOK and CHORUS:
Working on the clockwork plan, Tik-Tok.

(During song TIK-TOK moves automatically around.)

OZMA:
Perhaps this queer man can tell us which road to take.

<h1 style="text-align:center">ACT ONE, SCENE TWO</h1>

SHAGGY: *(To TIK-TOK)*
I want to find the way to the kingdom of the Metal Monarch.

TIK-TOK:
I know the ras-cal. He threw me in the well.

SHAGGY:
Well! Well!

TIK-TOK:
Be-cause my ma-chin-er-y would not do his wic-ked bid-ding.

SHAGGY:
Oh, wouldn't it?

TIK-TOK:
No; because the Me-tal Mon-arch is in-flu-enced by hate, and on-ly love can con-trol my mech-an-ism.

BETSY, OZMA, POLYCHROME:
Love!

TIK-TOK:
It's love that makes the wheels go round.

SHAGGY:
You mean the world go round.

TIK-TOK:
I mean what I say.

SHAGGY:
You're wrong.

ACT ONE, SCENE TWO

TIK-TOK:

I'm right ac-cor-ding to my ma-chin-er-y.

SHAGGY:

Tell us, then; which road leads to the Metal Kingdom.

TIK-TOK:

You take the gr-r-r—bib-i-kib-i-gig-a-chug-kik------

(As TIK-TOK mumbles incoherently all shrink away from him.)

POLYCHROME:

What's gone wrong now?

SHAGGY:

It's his think works. They've run down.

OZMA:

Wind him up, Betsy! Quick!

(As TIK-TOK continues to mumble, BETSY winds him under left arm.)

TIK-TOK:

Ma-ny thanks. Beg par-don for go-ing dip-py, but if a man's thoughts run down he's out of bus-i-ness.

SHAGGY:

Well, tell me before you go dead again, which road leads to the Metal Monarch's Kingdom?

TIK-TOK:

I won't.

SHAGGY:

No? Well, if love can influence your one-cylinder motion, I'll make you tell me.

(SHAGGY holds up Love Magnet. TIK-TOK at once advances and leans his head on SHAGGY's shoulder and chucks him under chin.)

TIK-TOK:

Toot-sie! Woot-sie!

SHAGGY:

Now, Tik-Tok, will you tell me the road to the Metal Monarch's Kingdom?

TIK-TOK:

I can't, honey love.

SHAGGY:

Why not?

TIK-TOK:

I don't know the road.

BETSY:

Hank knows as much as this junk heap. Don't you, Hank?

HANK:

Hee-haw! *(Prances up stage and points hoof along one of the roads.)*

SHAGGY:

Is that the way, Hank?

HANK:

Hee-haw!

ACT ONE, SCENE TWO

SHAGGY:

He wants us to hoof it.

BETSY:

Come on, folks. I told you Hank would know.

(ALL Exit. End of Scene Two.)

SCENE THREE - Field of Flowers. *(Music vamps until ARMY Enters.)*

Musical Number 8 – "The Army of Oogaboo" – QUEEN ANN, FILES, and ARMY

QUEEN ANN and (ARMY):

I'm the Queen of Oogaboo
And this here is my army;
I'll confide a fact to you,
No enemy can harm me.
We can conquer any land! (Hip! hip! hip! hip!)
We can fight to beat the band! (Hip! hip! hip! hip!)
Foemen see us, quickly flee us,
Ev'ryone would like to be us,
We're courageous through and through
And fight for Oogaboo, (Oogaboo!) for Oogaboo! (Oogaboo!)
(For Oogaboo! For Oogaboo!) For Oogaboo!

QUEEN ANN, FILES and (ARMY):

We are the army of Oogaboo, (Oogaboo, Oogaboo!)
We are the army of Oogaboo! (Oogoboo, Oogaboo!)
Pennants flying, foes defying,
Brave, undaunted, bold and true. (To Oogaboo)
For if we fight and run away, (runaway runaway)
Then we can fight another day, (fight another day)
That is why we always cry, Hurrah for Oogaboo! (boo! boo!)

ACT ONE, SCENE THREE

FILES and (ARMY):
(March, march, march, march,) On the march I be!
(No army in the universe can march as well as he!)
(Halt, halt, halt, halt,) Halted now I be.
(No army in the universe can halt as quick as he,
(As quick as he, can halt as quick, as quick as he, as quick as he, can halt as quick, as quick as he, as quick as he!)
(Can halt as quick as he, as quick he, can halt as quick, as quick, as he, as quick, as he, can halt as quick, as quick as he, as quick as he!)

FILES, QUEEN ANN and (ARMY):
We are the army of Oogaboo, (Oogoboo, Oogaboo!)
We are the army of Oogaboo! (Oogaboo, Oogaboo!)
Pennants flying, foes defying,
Brave, undaunted, bold and true, (and true, and true)
For if we fight and run away, (runaway runaway)
Then we can fight another day, (fight another day)
That is why we always cry; Hurrah for Oogaboo! (boo! boo!)

QUEEN ANN and (ARMY):
Blood's a dreadful thing to see
And so we never shed it;
Not a man would hurt a flea,
It's greatly to our credit.
Yet we are so fierce and grand, (Hip! hip! hip! hip!)
None against our might can stand! (Hip! hip! hip! hip!)
When advancing, weapons glancing,
We're a sight that's most entrancing,
Uniforms of gorgeous hue,
The pride of Oogaboo, (Oogaboo!) of Oogaboo!
(Oogaboo! Of Oogaboo! Of Oogaboo!) Of Oogaboo!

FILES, QUEEN ANN and (ARMY):
We are the army of Oogaboo, (Oogaboo, Oogaboo!)
We are the army of Oogaboo! (Oogaboo, Oogaboo!)
Pennants flying, foes defying,
Brave, undaunted, bold and true. (To Oogaboo)
For if we fight and run away, (runaway runaway)
Then we can fight another day, (fight another day)
That is why we always cry, Hurrah for Oogaboo! (boo! boo!)

QUEEN ANN of OOGABOO:
My brave boys, we've come all the way from home, seeking adventure, and your advent hasn't turned up any excitement so far.

PRIVATE FILES:
That's not my fault.

ANN:
Be respectful! Or I'll dock your pay.

FILES:
You can't dock mine, Your Majesty!

ANN:
Why not?

FILES:
Because I don't get any pay. All I get is promises. This life is not what I expected when I enlisted.

ANN:
What did you expect?

FILES:

War! Carnage! Devastation! Conflict and blood!

ANN:

But that would be wrong. If that's what you want, you ought to get a job in the stock-yards.

FILES:

I've had enough. I'm going to resign.

ANN:

You won't, Private Files. You're the only army we have, so you may as well be resigned to your fate, for it's the only resignation I'll accept. But there's another reason.

FILES:

What is it?

ANN:

You've won my heart, Private.

FILES:

A soldier's chief duty is to win the hearts of women. But I don't want it.

ANN:

I'm going to command you to marry me and become my royal consort.

FILES:

Where can you find another victim to take my place as private?

ANN:

Can't I hire another private?

ACT ONE, SCENE THREE

FILES:

You don't pay, so the job don't pay.

ANN:

Listen, then! Here we are in a foreign country. It looks prosperous, so we'll conquer it and divide the spoils.

OFFICERS:

Hurray!

ANN:

But you mustn't hurt anybody.

FILES: (Desperately)

I will! I will! I'll kill, slay, murder, butcher—anything for excitement!

ANN:

Why don't you marry me?

FILES:

I—I'm not brave enough.

ANN:

Obey orders, sir! Let us explore the enemy's territory!

(Exit ANN and ARMY, except for FILES.)

(FILES looks around stage, exploring the territory. As FILES bends over to examine some flowers, HANK enters and spots FILES picking a flower to smell. HANK approaches FILES quietly, turns around to kick FILES in his backside. FILES, alerted, turns to see HANK backing toward him. HANK chases FILES around the stage and off. Exit FILES and HANK.)

(Enter OZMA.)

ACT ONE, SCENE THREE

Musical Number 9 – "There's a Mate in This Big World for You"
– OZMA

OZMA:
In fancy's realm, in sweet repose,
I dreamed of gardens fair;
It seems that I was born a rose,
Of royalty so rare;
When Cupid with his little dart
Came flitting by, you see,
And with his arrow pierced my heart,
Then true love came to me;
I wish that I had Cupid's pow'r,
Do you know what I would do?
I'd take his darts and pierce the hearts
Of you, and you, and you.

When loves come stealing, to you appealing,
And knocking at your heart,
Do not embrace it, yet don't efface it,
But do decline, dear, love for a time, dear;
When love is fleeting, some fond heart's beating,
There's always some one to woo,
For someone is keeping his heart so true;
There's a mate in this big world for you.

If love should come to your rose bow'r
And that love proved untrue,
Then I'd resist Dan Cupid's pow'r,
That is, if I were you;
Another mate will come, 'tis fate,
The one you know is true;
If Cupid shoots his arrow straight,
True love will come to you;

I wish that I had Cupid's pow'r,
Do you know what I would do?
I'd take his darts and pierce the hearts
Of you, and you, and you.

When loves come stealing, to you appealing,
And knocking at your heart,
Do not embrace it, yet don't efface it,
But do decline, dear, love for a time, dear;
When love is fleeting, some fond heart's beating,
There's always some one to woo,
For someone is keeping his heart so true;
There's a mate in this big world for you.

(ENTER FILES.)

FILES:

Talk about warfare! I haven't seen anything fair since I've been in this business— *(Sees OZMA)* —until now!

OZMA:

Oh, I didn't know you were here!

FILES:

Your servant, fair one! *(Salutes.)*

OZMA:

I ceased to be a fairy when I was driven out of my Rose Kingdom and will never again be more than a mere mortal. But now I've lost all my friends.

FILES:

And found another! I'm Private Files of the Army of Oogaboo.

ACT ONE, SCENE THREE

OZMA:

I'm Princess Ozma of Roseland, but my subjects have driven me into exile because they wanted a man to rule over them.

FILES:

So lovely a blossom should have more devoted subjects; and, if your own forsake you, here is another, at your feet. *(Kneels.)*

OZMA:

My friends and I are seeking the way to the Metal Kingdom; but we don't know which road to take.

FILES:

Why don't you call upon your cousins to assist you?

OZMA: *(Wonderingly)*

My cousins?

FILES:

Are not the Field Flowers your cousins, humble though they may be? They must know where the roads lead to, for the Field Flowers have listened to travelers for ages.

Musical Number 10 – "Ask the Flowers to Tell You" – OZMA and FILES

FILES:

There's a little flow'ret,
Pretty little flow'ret!
Nestling in the meadow green;
Petals white and spreading,
Golden center wedding,
Daintier was never seen!

Lovers come to gather and to ask it whether
"She loves me or loves me not?"
Like a necromancer Daisy gives the answer;
Then the flow'r is soon forgot.

OZMA:

He loves me

FILES:

She loves me not! She loves me

OZMA:

He loves me not

BOTH:

Daisy leaf, pray tell me true:
Loves (s)he me? Oh, tell me do!

FILES:

She loves me

OZMA:

He loves me not! He loves me

FILES:

She loves me not!

BOTH:

Give me quick the answer, pray,
Loves (s)he me? oh, Daisy say!
Ask the flow'rs to tell you,
And they'll always tell you true;
They're the wisest little things
That mortals ever knew.

When you're puzzled or in doubt,
Just seek the clever blossoms out
And ask the flow'rs to tell you
For they'll always tell you true.

FILES:

In the meadow hiding,
Modest and confiding,
Grows the golden Buttercup;
Yellow hues reflecting,
When, its glow expecting,
To your chin you hold it up.
Seeing is believing, so it's not deceiving
When it tints your face with gold;
Blissfully assuring, happy and alluring
Is the message when it's told:
Buttercup, pray, let me see
If your test means joy for me!

OZMA:

Love you butter? Then you'll be
Fond and true eternally!

FILES:

This the sign well known of old:
If you love, reflect the gold!

OZMA:

But if not, a visage cold
O'er the flow'r I will behold!

BOTH:

Ask the flow'rs to tell you,
And they'll always tell you true;

They're the wisest little things
That mortals ever knew.
When you're puzzled or in doubt,
Just seek the clever blossoms out
And ask the flow'rs to tell you
For they'll always tell you true.

FILES:

You may ask the roses
When your love proposes:
"Is the answer Yes or No?"
He's no need to guess it,
For they'll quick confess it
By the color that they show.
In her hair reposes reddest of the roses
If the maid will answer "Yes,"
But a white rose choosing means she is refusing
And your suit you may not press.

OZMA:

Roses red have ever said
That the maid her love will wed;

FILES:

Roses white will Cupid fright,
Lovers all deplore the sight!

OZMA

So the maids with careless grace
In their hair the tokens place,

FILES:

And your fate you quickly see
"Yes" or "No" 'tis sure to be.

BOTH:

Ask the flow'rs to tell you,
And they'll always tell you true;
They're the wisest little things
That mortals ever knew.
When you're puzzled or in doubt,
Just seek the clever blossoms out
And ask the flow'rs to tell you
For they'll always tell you true.

(EXIT OZMA and FILES.)

(ENTER BETSY, HANK, SHAGGY, and TIK-TOK.)

HANK:

Hee-haw!

TIK-TOK:

How dread-ful!

BETSY:

Only at first. When you get used to it, it puts you to sleep. Hank's my mule—faithful and true, ain't you, Hank?

HANK: (Nuzzling BETSY)

Hee-haw!

BETSY:

I didn't need the Magnet to make you love me, did I?

SHAGGY:

He hasn't any Love Magnet.

ACT ONE, SCENE THREE

BETSY:

Oh, yes he has; there's a magnet on each hoof. *(Holds one up.)* That's why
I love him.

Musical Number 11 – "Dear Old Hank" – BETSY

BETSY:

There are many kinds of treasures,
There are many kinds of jew'ls;
There are many kinds of pleasures,
There are many kinds of mules.
There's the jackass, donkey, burro,
But I'll make a statement frank:
That you'll never find but one of a kind
Like dear old Hank!

A steed indeed is dear old Hank!
His pedigree is of the highest rank;
And tho' his bray you hear all day,
It's very safe to bank
That a jewel of a mu-el is dear old Hank!
That a jewel of a mu-el is dear old Hank!

There are many kinds of kickers,
You can meet 'em any day;
Other beasts with howls and bickers
Make us tired of their bray;
But in all my times of trouble
All my lucky stars I thank
That I have won a champion
Like dear old Hank!

A rum old chum is dear old Hank!
Though I'll admit he's rather lean and lank;

But none can fool this clever mule
Or dare his tail to yank,
Or he'd feel of the heel of dear old Hank!
Or he'd feel of the heel of dear old Hank!

(*ENTER ANN and OFFICERS of the ARMY OF OOGABOO.*)

ANN:

The private is a deserter. But although he has run away, my love for him remains.

SHAGGY:

Hello, what's this outfit?—banditti?

ANN:

I'm Queen Ann of Oogaboo—and this is my army—except there's no private.

TIK-TOK:

It's a pub-lic ar-my. "For-ward the tight bri-gade, charge for the drinks, he said!"

SHAGGY:

You're wrong. "Forward the light brigade—"

TIK-TOK:

I'm right ac-cor-ding to my ma-chin-er-y.

SHAGGY:

Your machinery's on the bum.

TIK-TOK:

Don't blame me—blame—z-z-z-z-z-z-z—the pa-ten-tee.

BETSY: (*To ANN*)

What's the good of an army in this forsaken place?

ACT ONE, SCENE THREE

ANN:

We're here to conquer the world.

SHAGGY:

I have an idea! I need this outfit to fight and conquer the Metal Monarch—

ANN:

Who's he?

SHAGGY:

Ruler of the underground Metal Kingdom.

ANN:

Is he rich?

SHAGGY:

Owns all the metal in the world—gold, silver, copper, iron, politicians, radium, tin, life-insurance agents, and brass.

ANN:

Good! We'll conquer him!

SHAGGY:

And release my dear brother from captivity!

ANN:

And with the booty, we'll pay my army all their arrears of salary!

OFFICERS:

Hurray!

OFFICER 1:

But we haven't any private soldier.

ACT ONE, SCENE THREE

OFFICER 2:

We need a private to command.

OFFICER 3:

So we can order him to fight our battles.

ANN: *(To SHAGGY)*

We must have a private soldier.

BETSY:

Make Tik-Tok the private.

SHAGGY:

Tik-Tok can't fight; he's only a bunch of old iron.

BETSY:

Yes, but he's scrap iron.

TIK-TOK:

I can't fight and I can't run!

BETSY:

You can if you're wound up, Tik-Tok!

ANN:

An ideal soldier!

TIK-TOK:

I refuse to fight.

SHAGGY:

What's the matter? Are you afraid?

TIK-TOK:
No. If I'm cap-tured there's an es-cape-ment in my clock-works.

BETSY: *(To ANN)*
He says his clockwork is only regulated by love. Pretend to love him and you'll win an army.

ANN: *(Approaches TIK-TOK)*
My darling Tik-Tok! Although I love another man in the flesh, you are the only clockwork individual I admire. Say you'll be my army and I'll swear never to love another machine as I do you.

TIK-TOK:
Fair Queen, you have won my cog-wheels! I ac-cept your of-fer!

OFFICERS:
Hurray!

(ENTER POLYCHROME, dancing gaily.)

POLYCHROME:
I found them!

ALL:
Whom?

POLYCHROME:
Princess Ozma and Private Files.

ANN:
Where were they?

POLYCHROME:
Kissing behind a rose-bush.

ACT ONE, SCENE THREE

SHAGGY:

If kisses left marks, some girls' faces would look like waffles.

TIK-TOK:

How scan-da-lous!

(Enter FILES and OZMA.)

FILES:

Not at all! I'm going to take the Army of Oogaboo to the Rose Kingdom, conquer the rebellious subjects, and marry the Princess.

ANN:

You're too late, my good man. Your resignation has been accepted, and this noble soldier *(Pointing to TIK-TOK)* is now the Army of Oogaboo.

SHAGGY:

We're going to conquer the Metal Kingdom and rescue my brother from the Metal Monarch. That is, we're going as soon as we discover the way.

FILES:

The Field Flowers will tell us the way.

Musical Number 12 –"Act One Finale" –PRINCIPALS and FIELD FLOWERS

POLYCHROME:
Prithee, little field-flowers,
Pretty little field-flowers,
Listen as we sing;
We have lost our way, so
Tell us how we may go
To the ringing Metal King.

ACT ONE, SCENE THREE

(Chorus of FIELD FLOWERS dances about stage, gradually forming them-selves into a line diagonally across stage.)

FIELD FLOWER 1:

There lies the way,
So have no hesitation.

FIELD FLOWER 2:

There lies the way
Unto your destination.

FIELD FLOWER 3:

The Metal Monarch you will find
To strangers ever most unkind;

FIELD FLOWER 4:

But if to dangers you are blind,

ALL PRINCIPALS AND FIELD FLOWERS: *(Unison)*

There lies the way.

(FIELD FLOWERS point along their diagonal line.)

FILES:

Oh, now we know which way to go.
These beauties show us clearly, so
We'll make a start
And all depart
With courage smart and cheerful heart.

ANN:

No more we dwell beneath a spell.
These flowers tell us very well

The very thing
We need to bring
Us to the metal king.

FILES and ANN: *(Unison)*
Then forward, march to victory!

TIK-TOK:
Yes, I am marching, can't you see?

SHAGGY:
We'll take a stand
'Gainst the Metal Monarch and
We'll set my brother free!

BETSY:

To victory!

(One by one they march along the diagonal line, first HANK and POLY-CHROME, then FILES, ANN, TIK-TOK, SHAGGY, and BETSY, who is last.)

ALL:
So march away to victory; to victory!
We love the fray, we're brave and free;
The breath of life
Is war and strife
To soldiers such as we!

BETSY:

To victory!

(As they EXIT, including ARMY OF OOGABOO and FIELD FLOWERS, TIK-TOK runs down and suddenly stops, still on stage, while others EXIT.)

ACT ONE, SCENE THREE

TIK-TOK: *(Alone on stage as music continues to play)*
Help! Wind-me-up-wind-me-up-wind-me-up—

(BETSY runs back on and winds him on chest. Exit BETSY, followed by TIK-TOK, who with awkward movements runs into wings, backs out, turns abrupt corners, and finally marches out.)

END OF ACT ONE

MUSICAL NUMBER 13 – ENTR'ACTE – THE TIK-TOK MAN OF OZ "LANCIERS"

ACT TWO

SCENE ONE—The Metal Monarch's Underground Cavern - This scene consists of an irregular rock setting. Perched upon rocks in various places is the chorus of METAL IMPS, engaged in hammering upon anvils in accompaniment to the musical number. At center of cavern is the METAL MONARCH, RUGGEDO, wearing his Magic Belt. When the METAL MONARCH wishes to perform any magic trick, he pushes the proper button on the belt, and a bell rings to indicate that the magic has been performed.

Musical Number 14 – "Work, Lads, Work" – RUGGEDO and METAL IMPS

RUGGEDO:
Work, lads, work! Don't let me catch you lagging:
Work, lads, work! With spirit never flagging!
You've got a lot of things to do
Before you quit, I promise you,
There'll be no rest till you are through
So work, lads, work! So work, lads, work!

METAL IMPS:
We're making spirit cabinets to fool the human race,
And muzzles for your moth'r-in-law to wear upon her face:
Our thirst producers are so fine we cannot make enough:
Our corset steels and French high heels to torture are the stuff.

RUGGEDO:
Work, lads, work, you've got to keep a-going!
Work, lads, work! And set the forges glowing!
Our orders you must promptly fill,
Because our products fill the bill,

So heave your hammers with a will, and work, lads, work!
So heave your hammers with a will, and work, lads, work!

METAL IMPS:
We will work because we must, raining mighty blows and just,
Bellows blowing, forges glowing, labor is the common lot.
We are hardy, sturdy, bold, beating out the gleaming gold;
Sparks a-flying, fire defying, striking while the metal's hot!
(Ding, Dong, Ding, Dong, Ding, Dong, Ding, Dong, Ding, Dong, Ding,
Dong, Ding, Dong, Ding, Dong, Ding, Dong, Ding, Dong, Ding, Dong,
Ding, Dong, Ding, Dong, Ding Dong, Ding, Dong, Dong.)

RUGGEDO:
So heave your hammers with a will and work, lads, work, rah!

Work, lads, work! For vengeance and for glory;
Work, lads, work! Each blow will tell its story!
We'll forge the shackles for mankind,
Whose lust for metal makes 'em blind;
Their fate is in our net entwined,
So work, lads, work! So work, lads, work!

METAL IMPS:
He's known to be a wicked king and foe to human kind;
No one so very wicked in this universe you'll find;
From love and sentiment he turns, to strive for hate alone;
His conscience never troubles him, so wicked has he grown.

RUGGEDO:
Smite, lads, smite the gold so cold and yielding,
Clash and crash! Your hammers nobly wielding;
And let your anvils sing the song
Of all our staunch and mighty throng.

The profits all to me belong, so smite, lads, smite!
The profits all to me belong, so smite, lads, smite!

METAL IMPS:
We will work because we must, raining mighty blows and just,
Bellows blowing, forges glowing, labor is the common lot.
We are hardy, sturdy, bold, beating out the gleaming gold;
Sparks a-flying, fire defying, striking while the metal's hot!
(Ding, Dong, Ding, Dong, Ding, Dong, Ding, Dong, Ding, Dong, Ding,
Dong, Ding, Dong, Ding, Dong, Ding, Dong, Ding, Dong, Ding, Dong,
Ding, Dong, Ding, Dong, Ding Dong, Ding, Dong, Dong.)

RUGGEDO:
The profits all to me belong so smite, lads, smite, rah!

(At end of number, IMPS Exit so that RUGGEDO is alone on stage.)

(Enter POLYCHROME.)

RUGGEDO:
Hello, what's up now, or rather down? There can't be a rainbow underground! Im-possible!

POLYCHROME:
Are we not welcome, Ruggedo?

RUGGEDO:
No; I hate all mortals because they rob my kingdom of its gold and precious metals. If they keep on digging, they'll bankrupt me!

POLYCHROME:
But I'm not a mortal. I'm the daughter of the Rainbow. Don't you think
you could make an exception in my case?

RUGGEDO:

Perhaps; if I knew how to love. Can't you give me a lesson, little rainbow? If I once got started, I believe I could love frantically—furiously—distractedly!

POLYCHROME:

On the Rainbow love means happiness, a merry heart, and contentment. When I lived there I loved only my father and went to him in all my troubles.

RUGGEDO:

Is that one of the privileges of love?

POLYCHROME:

I think so.

RUGGEDO:

When in trouble come to Papa, eh?

POLYCHROME:

Yes; that's the idea.

MUSICAL NUMBER 15 – "WHEN IN TROUBLE COME TO PAPA" – RUGGEDO and POLYCHROME

RUGGEDO:
Oh! there's a friend that never fails you,
Comforts you whatever ails you;
At the restaurant regales you
In a lordly way.

POLYCHROME:
Or if your tailor gown don't fit you,
If your rivals all outwit you,
If the handsome chaps forget you,
There is one who'll say:

ACT TWO, SCENE ONE

BOTH:

When in trouble come to Papa!
He will see you through,
If you are an old man's darling,
To you he'll be true,
If your youthful lover quarrels,
If you're feeling blue,
Take your troubles all to Papa,
He will see you through.

POLYCHROME:

Oh! Papa never dares to bore you,
But declares he'll just adore you;
Dangles jewels bright before you
In a merry way.

RUGGEDO:

And all he asks is smiles and kisses,
Which a damsel never misses,
Your companionship his bliss is,
And he'll always say:

BOTH:

When in trouble come to Papa!
He will see you through,
If you are an old man's darling,
To you he'll be true,
If you find you're out of money,
And your board bill's due,
Take your troubles all to Papa,
He will see you through.

(ENTER *SHAGGY MAN, ANN, TIK-TOK, BETSY, HANK, and OFFICERS of the ARMY OF OOGABOO.*)

SHAGGY:

We've reached the Kingdom of the Metal Monarch at last, and our first business is to conquer him.

RUGGEDO:

Clash and clatter! What's the meaning of this invasion?

SHAGGY:

We've come to release my brother, whom you captured in our Colorado mine.

RUGGEDO:

The Ugly Man! Im-possible! Why, his face would stop a clock!

TIK-TOK:

Then don't re-lease him. My clock stops too of-ten now!

BETSY: *(to SHAGGY)*

Why do they call him the Ugly Man?

SHAGGY:

I don't know. *(He attempts a handsome pose.)* All of our family are noted for their handsome faces.

RUGGEDO:

I performed an enchantment. I made him ugly in the eyes of all the world. Now, away with you—vacate at once, or I'll make you all my slaves!

ANN:

Sir, I declare war upon you and your whole kingdom. I'm Queen Ann of Oogaboo—and this is my invincible army! *(Indicates TIK-TOK)* We've come here to conquer you.

RUGGEDO:

Very well, have your own way. *(He yawns.)*

ACT TWO, SCENE ONE

Musical Number 16 – "Fight for Oogaboo" - ANN and OFFICERS of the ARMY of OOGABOO

ANN:

Now my men of Oogaboo,
Pitch in and do your duty;
Teach the Metal King who's who
And capture all his booty;
You're invincible and bold—

OFFICERS: (Marking time.)

Hip! Hip! Hip! Hip!

ANN:

Strike to win both fame and gold—

OFFICERS:

Hip! hip! hip! hip!

ANN and (OFFICERS):

You will fright 'em when you fight 'em,
Swing your swords and bravely smite 'em,
You will conquer if you do,
So fight for Oogaboo, (Oogaboo!) for Oogaboo! (Oogaboo!)

OFFICERS:

We are the army of Oogaboo, Oogaboo—
We are the army of Oogaboo, Oogaboo—
Never flying, foes defying,
Brave, undaunted, bold and true. To Oogaboo,
Now we are on this contest bent, Oogaboo—
And if we win we are content, Oogaboo—
So look out when we all shout:
Hurrah for Oogaboo! boo! boo!

(OFFICERS wave swords.)

RUGGEDO:

Wait a minute, till I summon my army! *(He pushes a button on his Magic Belt. A bell rings.)* Ah, I pushed the wrong button. That's the signal to light the furnaces. *(He pushes another button. Bell rings and clash of metal is heard.)* Another mistake! The tin mine has caved in. *(Looks at buttons on Magic Belt in confusion.)* Which button summons my army?

ANN:

Hurry up. We want to fight!

TIK-TOK:

I have-n't an-y wea-pons.

ANN:

Never mind. Use your fists.

RUGGEDO:

The north-east button. I'm sure I'm right. *(RUGGEDO pushes button and a bell rings.)*

(The METAL IMPS appear in different parts of the stage, bearing great golden shields and zig-zag swords. The PRINCIPALS are gathered at center.)

MUSICAL NUMBER 17 – "IMPS MARCH"

(METAL IMPS perform a precision march. At end of dance the METAL IMPS have surrounded the PRINCIPALS and ARMY OF OOGABOO in a half circle stretching from one side of the stage to the other.)

RUGGEDO:

Now I'm ready, whenever you are.

ACT TWO, SCENE ONE

OFFICER 1:

Attention!

OFFICER 2:

Advance!

OFFICER 3:

Double-quick!

ALL OFFICERS:

March!

(TIK-TOK walks forward a few steps then suddenly stops.)

TIK-TOK:

Wind-me-up-wind-me-up-wind-me-up-wind----

ANN:

Quick! Polly!

(POLYCHROME runs forward and winds TIK-TOK on chest.)

TIK-TOK:

Ma-ny thanks.

OFFICER 4:

Summon the Metal Monarch to surrender!

TIK-TOK: *(To RUGGEDO)*

Sir, I summon you to sur-reg-ge-doo-bug-a-rug-a-dug-boo-dle—

BETSY:

Now his thoughts have run down!

ACT TWO, SCENE ONE

ANN:

Quick, Polly!

(POLYCHROME winds TIK-TOK up under left arm.)

SHAGGY:

Tik-Tok, you're a bum soldier. Hurry up and conquer.

TIK-TOK:

I'm try-ing to. If I on-ly had a—*(Stops short and waves arms wildly.)*

(POLYCHROME winds TIK-TOK under right arm.)

RUGGEDO:

Enough! You've had your chance to fight. Now it's my turn. To conquer my imps is im-possible! You are defeated already, so I call on you to sur-render.

(METAL IMPS advance threateningly.)

SHAGGY:

There's a power greater than your own—the power of Cupid! *(SHAGGY takes Love Magnet out and holds it up.)* I command all your imps to love me!

(METAL IMPS all kneel before SHAGGY and lower their swords.)

SHAGGY:

You see, unfortunate monarch, you are defeated!

RUGGEDO:

Im-possible! There's one shot still left in this Magic Belt. All I have to do is press a button and every mortal present will become powerless.

(RUGGEDO touches button, bell rings. ANN, SHAGGY, BETSY, HANK, and OFFICERS all become motionless in their places. METAL IMPS rise and EXIT.)

POLYCHROME:

Dear me; what is the matter with them?

RUGGEDO:

Hello? You're not mortal, my pretty maid.

POLYCHROME:

No, Your Majesty. But what has happened to our friends?

RUGGEDO:

The neatest magic trick my wonderful Magic Belt can accomplish. It's a case of arrested animation. I've stopped their clocks, so to speak. They can't think, speak or move till I release 'em.

TIK-TOK:

You have-n't stopped my clock.

RUGGEDO:

No; you're not mortal. But you'll soon run down.

TIK-TOK: *(Slowly)*

I feel—sort-a-------run down------------now.

POLYCHROME:

But tell me, Ruggedo. How can you release our friends, should you wish to?

RUGGEDO:

By pressing this last button on the left. *(Pointing)* See? Until I press that button, your friends will be ornamental—but not useful.

ACT TWO, SCENE ONE

POLYCHROME:

Your Majesty, this is cruel and unjust.

RUGGEDO:

Im-possible! For years these mortals have been robbing my dominions of all its gold, and now they have the audacity to penetrate to my Royal Cavern. I hate 'em! I hate everybody—but you, sweet Polychrome!

POLYCHROME:

Listen, Ruggedo. I know where there is enough gold to repay you for all that the mortals have stolen.

RUGGEDO: *(Eagerly)*

Where? Where?

POLYCHROME:

Wouldn't you be satisfied with the pot of gold at the rainbow's end?

RUGGEDO:

Yes, indeed!

POLYCHROME:

If you'll release these mortals, I'll show you where the gold is.

RUGGEDO:

I'll release them when I get the gold.

POLYCHROME:

Not before?

RUGGEDO:

Not a minute before. Tell me; when is the next rainstorm, my dear; and when will the next rainbow appear?

<h1 style="text-align:center">ACT TWO, SCENE ONE</h1>

POLYCHROME:

Look, Your Majesty! Look at the sky through the rocks yonder! *(Points.)* Do you see the storm approaching?

(RUGGEDO raises his head to look and POLYCHROME touches the button at the left of his Magic Belt. A bell rings and all the mortals waken to life, HANK capering about as if glad to be free.)

RUGGEDO: *(Furious)*

Hammer and tongs! What have you done, girl?

ANN:

Caught you in your own trap, Ruggedo! Now, officers, obey or you are lost. Form ranks! *(OFFICERS fall in line.)* Attention! *(OFFICERS draw swords.)* Forward, double-quick—march!

(OFFICERS surround RUGGEDO and two of them seize his arms.)

OFFICERS:

Hurrah!

ANN:

Don't let him touch his belt buttons.

RUGGEDO:

So I'm a prisoner, eh?

POLYCHROME:

Good people, this Metal Monarch is not so wicked as he seems. Let us compromise with him and be friends.

ANN:

How compromise?

POLYCHROME:

Mortals have stolen a lot of gold from the Metal Monarch. So I will show him how to get back an equal amount of gold from the pot at the rainbow's end—on certain conditions.

RUGGEDO:

State your conditions, my dear.

POLYCHROME:

First: you must release the Ugly Man, the Shaggy Man's brother.

RUGGEDO:

Agreed! He's of no use to me because he's too lazy to work. Let the Shaggy Man have his ugly brother, if he wants him.

SHAGGY:

Hurrah! *(Dances gleefully.)*

POLYCHROME:

Then you must give these officers enough gold to pay their back salaries.

RUGGEDO:

Im-possible!

TIK-TOK:

Then you must re-main our pri-son-er.

RUGGEDO:

Well—agreed!

OFFICERS:

Hurrah!

POLYCHROME:

And the last condition both you and Queen Ann must agree to—you must march with all your armies to the Rose Kingdom and force Ozma's rebellious subjects to accept her as their Queen—and Private Files as her Royal Consort.

ANN:

Why so?

POLYCHROME:

Because this is a case of true love, and everyone is bound to assist true lovers.

RUGGEDO:

Agreed!

ANN:

Agreed!

RUGGEDO:

Now, I've one condition to make myself. Polychrome must consent to marry me.

POLYCHROME:

My home, Ruggedo, is far up in the skies, while yours is far down in the earth caverns.

RUGGEDO:

That doesn't matter. Among these mortals, some husbands and wives are farther apart than that.

POLYCHROME:

I don't mind. I'd like to reform you. It's so interesting to reform a wicked husband. But I'll do it from my rainbow.

RUGGEDO:

I couldn't live on a rainbow.

ACT TWO, SCENE ONE

POLYCHROME:

No; you'll stay down below and worship me from afar.

Musical Number 18 – "Rainbow Bride" – POLYCHROME with RUG-

GEDO, ANN, SHAGGY, BETSY, and TIK-TOK

POLYCHROME:

If a youth adores a damsel
Who beyond his reach is placed,
Ev'ry charm the maid possesses
Is by distance doubly graced.
To him ev'ry smile is radiant,
Ev'ry glance a dart of flame;
Ev'ry blush is like a sunset:
Form and features Venus shame.

She is a rainbow of bliss to him
And marvelous fair she seems.
While from afar he worships his star—
The goddess of all his dreams.
Never a flaw in the gem he sees,
She is his joy and pride;
The queen of his heart, though far apart
She is his Rainbow Bride.

Woe to him if she draws nearer!
He will find her mortal clay.
Should he see her closer, clearer,
He'll forever rue the day.
Distance lends enchantment, surely,
When a hopeless lover sighs;
All his dreams are rainbow tinted—
She's perfection in his eyes.

CHORUS:
She is a rainbow of bliss to him
And marvelous fair she seems.
While from afar he worships his star—
The goddess of all his dreams.
Never a flaw in the gem he sees,
She is his joy and pride;
The queen of his heart, though far apart,
She is his Rainbow Bride.

(POLYCHROME sings first verse, chorus, and second verse. ALL sing chorus again after second verse.)

RUGGEDO:
And now we'll march away to the Metal Forest.

SHAGGY:
Where is that?

RUGGEDO:
It's in another part of my kingdom. It is in the Metal Forest that your brother is imprisoned.

POLYCHROME:
And on the way we will surely find the rainbow.

ANN:
And the pot of gold.

(Exit RUGGEDO, POLYCHROME, BETSY, HANK, and OFFICERS.)

ANN:
Halt! Where's Ozma? And where is Ex-private Files?

ACT TWO, SCENE ONE

SHAGGY:

Lost!

ANN:

Humbug!

SHAGGY:

They seemed lost—in mushy conversation. Anyhow, they're so busy they couldn't hurry.

TIK-TOK:

They'll soon be here. Love is a gr-r-r-r--- *(Waves arms wildly)*

ANN: *(Sarcastically)*
Oh, wind him up, so we can find out what love is.

SHAGGY:

Where's the key?

ANN:

It's hanging on his back.

  (SHAGGY winds TIK-TOK.)

TIK-TOK:

Ma-ny thanks!

SHAGGY:

Now, old fellow, the Queen wants to know what love is.

TIK-TOK:

She'll ne-ver find out.

ANN:

I know already. I love—*(throws herself at SHAGGY and clings to him)*—but thee!

SHAGGY:

Help, somebody! Help! *(He escapes ANN's grasp and hides behind TIK-TOK)*

TIK-TOK:

It's the Love Mag-net. You worked the charm once too of-ten.

SHAGGY: *(Sadly)*

You're right, I believe I have.

(SHAGGY stands a little back of TIK-TOK, takes out the Love Magnet, kisses it, and hangs it on a hook on TIK-TOK's back, without the Clockwork Man seeing him.)

SHAGGY:

Now, my energetic Queen, I'm free!

ANN:

Beautiful Tik-Tok! Exquisite creature! I love but thee!

(ANN throws herself upon TIK-TOK, who nearly tumbles over.)

TIK-TOK:

What's the joke?

ANN:

I love you, my armored crusader! You have the Love Magnet.

TIK-TOK: *(Turning around)*

Where is it?

SHAGGY: *(Gleefully)*

On your back—out of reach!

<h1 style="text-align:center">ACT TWO, SCENE ONE</h1>

ANN: *(To TIK-TOK)*

Can't you pay a little attention to me?

TIK-TOK:

We're pay-ing as lit-tle as pos-si-ble.

SHAGGY: *(To ANN)*

Look here, Ann, this is no time for love. All we want is to find the Metal Forest.

ANN:

Love will find a way! Forward, march!

(EXIT ANN, marching, TIK-TOK, and SHAGGY. End of Scene One.)

SCENE TWO - CAVES AND CHASM. *(ENTER FILES.)*

FILES: *(Despondently)*

Misfortune follows misfortune. My Rose Princess and I cannot have the assistance of the Army of Oogaboo and the Metal Imps until we've found the Metal Forest and liberated the Shaggy Man's brother. And the Metal Forest can't be found. Even the Metal Monarch has lost his way. So I must curb my impatience until the time comes when I may claim my lovely Rose.

MUSICAL NUMBER 19 – "MY WONDERFUL DREAM GIRL" – FILES

FILES:

Each night there's a wonderful face, so it seems,
That haunts me and taunts me in all of my dreams,
With a smile that is sadness and gladness combined
And two eyes that are very unruly.

ACT TWO, SCENE TWO

I try to forget you, but always at night
I see your sweet face, then I know well my plight,
My poor heart's afire with burning desire,
I love you, my wonderful dream girl.

Dream girl, dream girl, my life is lonely,
Dream girl, dream girl, without you near.
I love you dearly and so sincerely,
You'll be in life, dear, my dream girl wife dear,
I love you, my wonderful dream girl.

At night when the dream Gods are romping in play
And casting a spell which turns night into day,
A vision is there with wond'rous hair
And a form that is Venus truly.
I know ev'ry glance, I know ev'ry curl,
I can feel your embrace, my head's in a whirl,
I want to caress you, I dream I possess you,
I love you, my wonderful dream girl.

Dream girl, dream girl, my life is lonely,
Dream girl, dream girl, without you near.
I love you dearly and so sincerely,
You'll be in life, dear, my dream girl wife dear,
I love you, my wonderful dream girl.

(EXIT FILES.)

(ENTER TIK-TOK, who runs down and stands motionless.)

TIK-TOK:
Wind-me-up-wind-me-up-wind-me-up---

(ENTER BETSY and SHAGGY. BETSY winds TIK-TOK on chest.)

ACT TWO, SCENE TWO

SHAGGY:

Now look here, old man, if you run down again, I'm going to pound you into mince meat.

TIK-TOK:

You'd ruin my—z-z-z-z-z—ma-chin-er-y.

BETSY:

Your machinery is old and worn out. It's folly to waste time winding you up.

TIK-TOK:

Fol-ly is the jol-li-est thing in life.

SHAGGY:

There's some sense in that, old man.

MUSICAL NUMBER 20 – "FOLLY!" – TIK-TOK, BETSY, and SHAGGY

TIK-TOK and (ALL):

I wants to hike to Omaha, to seek the saucy lassie;
(Nicodemus!)
A tender, juicy roast of rump she eats up quick and sassy;
(Sacramento!)
I don'ts know were it biled or fried, or salted likes a noodle;
I only know this tasty treat's no longer in my boodle;
(Tooti frooti!)
No matter! Never mind! Such kindness is unkind!

ALL:

Folly! Folly! Isn't folly jolly?
Good for sunburn, freckles, warts,
Good for grouches, too!
Cholly! Molly! Cut out melancholy;
Take a whirl at folly!

ACT TWO, SCENE TWO

BETSY and (ALL):
The course of true love is, of course, a *table d'hote* in courses;
(Turn the gas low!)
To bet a bit of bood you'd better back the biggest horses;
(Soak your soaklets!)
The girl who has the votelet votes the vut that vix us trouble;
Her hatpin gives a stablet in your slabs that makes you double;
(You're the victim!)
A maid is made to fade the lollipop brigade!

ALL:
Folly! Folly! Isn't folly jolly?
Good for sunburn, freckles, warts,
Good for grouches, too!
Cholly! Molly! Cut out melancholy;
Take a whirl at folly!

SHAGGY and (ALL):
The baker boke a loaf of bread to feed the fedless loafer;
(What's the answer?)
The shofer showfed a shif that ought to shuffed the auto's shofer;
(There's a reason!)
When fighters fit the type machines they box their blocks with reason:
And then they vode a vid of vud in vaudeville a season;
(Curb your anguish!)
A beer can bore a bum! Its foam fims fumes of fum!

ALL:
Folly! Folly! Isn't folly jolly?
Good for sunburn, freckles, warts,
Good for grouches, too!
Cholly! Molly! Cut out melancholy;
Take a whirl at folly!

<h1 style="text-align:center">ACT TWO, SCENE TWO</h1>

(DANCE.)

(ENTER RUGGEDO.)

SHAGGY:

Don't you know the way to your own Metal Forest?

RUGGEDO:

Certainly. The Magic Belt always opens for me an underground passage. I just touch this button—so! *(Touches button. No bell.)* and the passage opens!

BETSY:

Only it don't!

SHAGGY:

That's all you're good for—talk!

BETSY: *(To RUGGEDO)*

Why don't you do something?

TIK-TOK:

You're a brass lob-ster!

RUGGEDO:

Crash and clatter! Give me a chance, won't you? Something's gone wrong. Ever since Tik-Tok loaned me the Love Magnet, this blamed old belt re-fuses to work. I can touch every dod-gasted button on it—and nothing happens! *(Touches buttons. No bells ring.)*

BETSY:

Perhaps love's more powerful than a Magic Belt.

TIK-TOK:

Es-pe-cial-ly if the ma-gic won't work.

SHAGGY:

What did you want of the Love Magnet? *(Points to the magnet, which is stuck in RUGGEDO's belt.)*

RUGGEDO:

I want to use it on Polychrome. A rainbow bride in the skies don't suit me. I want her in a more handy location—see?

TIK-TOK:

Poor Pol-ly!

SHAGGY:

Then what are we to do? Where's your old Metal Forest, anyhow?

RUGGEDO:

It must be just across this chasm.

SHAGGY:

That's sar-casm.

RUGGEDO:

Let me think! *(Places hands over eyes and stands silent. BETSY steals the Love Magnet from the Belt.)*

BETSY: *(Holding Love Magnet concealed behind her.)*
If the rainbow would appear over the canyon, we could bridge it.

RUGGEDO:

If you bridge it, I'll make it hearts. And that reminds me—I've lost Polychrome. *(Looks off.)* Ah! there she is!

(Exit RUGGEDO.)

ACT TWO, SCENE TWO

BETSY:

I've got it, boys! *(Holds up Love Magnet.)*

SHAGGY: *(Kneeling)*

Adorable Betsy! I love you!

TIK-TOK:

Be-witch-ing Bet-sy! I am yours!

SHAGGY:

You're not! Out of the way, cog-wheels!

TIK-TOK:

She's mine!

SHAGGY:

She's mine—ain't you, Betsy?

HANK

Hee-haw! *(HANK advances threateningly to protect BETSY. Comedy business with HANK chasing SHAGGY and TIK-TOK back and forth across the stage.)*

BETSY:

I'm my own, just now. Fight it out among yourselves, and if either of you wins me, just send me a wireless!

(Exit BETSY to one side. Exit SHAGGY MAN and TIK-TOK, chased off by HANK, to the other side.)

(Enter FILES and OZMA.)

OZMA:

Sweetheart, will you see your rose wither away and die in this dreary canyon?

ACT TWO, SCENE TWO

FILES:

Don't be downcast, dear one. Every cloud has a silver lining.

OZMA:

But we can't go to my own kingdom until we've found the Metal Forest, and this place is so cold and cheerless that not a flower can live here.

FILES:

Be brave a little longer, my darling. Love is a curious thing, and some consider it a remedy for all ills.

Musical Number 21 – "Oh! Take Me" – OZMA and FILES

OZMA:

It isn't very pleasing to have a fellow teasing,
Then try to be appeasing so gently.
When he's the one attraction that drives you to distraction,
You look for satisfaction intently.

FILES:

If you'll listen to my pleading, I'll give to you unheeding
The love you say you're needing so true, dear.
While you hold me in love's spell, there's a secret, dear, I'll tell,
Trusting you to guard it well, it's *Entre Nous*, dear.
I've named a sweet gift for you, queen,
My sweetheart's limousine.

OZMA:

Oh! take me, please, take me
Any place you want to go.
Oh! make me, just make me
Happy, for I love you so,
How much I love you'll never know.

Then wed me, yes, wed me,
That is what you ought to do,
For I will be your honey, dear,
And I will bank the money,
For I think an awful lot of you,
You can bet your little life I do.

You offer your protection, to which I've no objection,
You tender me affection so sweetly.
You say I'll bear inspection, you jolly my complexion,
But you don't pop the question discreetly.

FILES:
If you'll follow my direction through life without exception,
I'll promise no deception, you know, dear.
For I've found a rendezvous that is big enough for two,
It was built, my dear, for you, now will you go, dear?
We'll call it something apropos,
My sweetheart's bungalow.

OZMA:
Oh! take me, please, take me
To your little bungalow.
Oh! make me, just make me
Happy, for I love you so,
How much I love, you'll never know.
Then wed me, yes, wed me,
That is what you ought to do,
For you can do the ruling,
Honest, honey, I'm not fooling
For I think an awful lot of you,
You can bet your little life I do.

FILES:

We must stand together, my darling, for all the world's against us.

OZMA:

Oh, if all the world is Private Files, I—I don't mind it.

FILES:

Be careful, young woman! Caution is the watch-word. In days of old, girls were taught what was strictly proper; while the girls of today—

OZMA:

The girls of today aren't so strict—but they have a good time, just the same.

FILES:

We mortals pay many a forfeit just for fun.

OZMA:

It's better to suffer remorse than to miss a good time.

Musical Number 22 – "Just for Fun" – OZMA and FILES

FILES:

I know all about you.

OZMA:

Tell me what you've heard!

FILES:

People seem to doubt you

OZMA:

Isn't that absurd!
Tell me what they're saying!

<h1 align="center">ACT TWO, SCENE TWO</h1>

FILES:
Secrets they're betraying;

OZMA:
Jealousy displaying with each spiteful word.

FILES:

Gossips are asserting, and they all agree,
That you kissed, in flirting, a man with manner free!

OZMA:

Such a horried slander rouses all my my dander;
I insist with candor, 'twas the man kissed me!

BOTH:

And really, no one ever misses such a thing as kisses;
That's the reason this is apropos!
Just a little squeezing, love's desire appeasing,
Is so very pleasing.
No! No! No! (Don't say no!)

FILES:

Girls are gay deceivers.

OZMA:
I've heard that before!

FILES:

Men are true believers;

OZMA:
What an awful bore;

If a girl's vivacious, very sweet and gracious,
She is called flirtatious.

ACT TWO, SCENE TWO

FILES:

Flirting I adore!
Dine with me tonight, dear!

OZMA:

I don't drink, you see.

FILES:

We will have a bite, dear.

OZMA:

Love must hungry be!
You seem fond of flirting.

FILES:

Yes, it's so diverting.

OZMA:

But it's disconcerting when you're stringing me!

BOTH:

We all know flirting is alluring, gaiety assuring,
Happiness securing, on the run;
Though it's merely jesting, it is interesting,
Wiles and smiles suggesting, just for fun!

(DANCE.)

FILES:

When we've found this wonderful Metal Forest, if we ever do, you shall
have the army of Oogaboo to assist you in conquering your wild roses. If
only I could manage to cross this chasm, I believe the Metal Forest would
not be far distant. Be brave, my sweet Rose!

ACT TWO, SCENE TWO

(ENTER POLYCHROME from one side. ENTER SHAGGY, TIK-TOK, QUEEN ANN, BETSY, and HANK from the other side.)

POLYCHROME:

Quick, friends—quick! A storm is coming!

SHAGGY:

Let 'er come—we can't help it.

POLYCHROME:

But it will be followed by the rainbow.

ALL: *(Wonderingly)*

The Rainbow!

POLYCHROME:

Yes; it will span the canyon, and if you are quick, you can cross on it before it lifts.

BETSY:

We'll try, Polly, dear!

INCIDENTAL MUSIC 23 – DANCE OF THE RAINBOWS FROM "OH! MY BOW"

(Rainbow appears.)

POLYCHROME: *(Raising her arms)*

Help us, dear father!

(ALL—including OFFICERS of the ARMY OF OOGABOO, if desired—cross over Rainbow and EXIT.)

(ENTER RUGGEDO.)

ACT TWO, SCENE TWO

RUGGEDO:

They all crossed the gulch on the rainbow. I've lost the precious Love Magnet.

*   *   *   *   *

(The following dialogue and song for RUGGEDO are optional. They may be omitted from performance by skipping ahead to RUGGEDO's dialogue immediately following the next row of asterisks.)

RUGGEDO: *(continued)*

Have I also lost Polychrome? I'd give half my kingdom to get her back. Perhaps I'd do better to wipe her from my memory. But how can such a ray of loveliness ever be forgotten?

Optional Musical Number 23-B – "Forgotten" – RUGGEDO

RUGGEDO:

Forgotten you? Well, if forgetting
Be thinking all the day
How the long hours drag since you left me—
(Days seem years with you away.)
Or hearing through all the strange babble
Of voices, now grave, now gay,
Only your voice: Can this be forgetting?
Yet I have forgotten, you say.
Or counting each moment with longing,
Till the one when I'll see you again.
If this be forgetting, you're right, dear,
And I have forgotten you, then.

Forgotten you? Well, if forgetting
Be reading each face that I see
With eyes that mark never a feature,
Save yours as you last looked at me.

Forgotten you? Well, if forgetting
Be yearning with all my heart,
With a longing, half pain and half rapture,
For the time when we never shall part.
If the wild wish to see you and hear you,
To be held in your arms again,
If this be forgetting, you're right, dear,
And I have forgotten you, then.
Forgotten, you say!

(End of optional dialogue and song.)

* * * * *

RUGGEDO: *(continued)*
But having seen Polychrome, and having once possessed the Love Magnet, I shall never be happy again without the girl or the charm to win her. I'll have my sweet Polychrome—if I have to follow her to the rainbow.

(RUGGEDO crosses over Rainbow and Exits. End of Scene Two.)

SCENE THREE – The Metal Forest – The trees are all made of various metals, silver predominating.

(BETSY, HANK, and OZMA are discovered on stage as scene opens. TIK-TOK lies in a broken heap.)

(Enter RUGGEDO.)

OZMA:
What a beautiful forest, Ruggedo.

RUGGEDO:
Yes, it has amused us for years in the making.

<h1>ACT TWO, SCENE THREE</h1>

OZMA:

It must be worth a lot of money.

RUGGEDO:

I don't care for money. All I love to possess is the metal itself. But listen, I'll give the most precious tree in this forest for the Love Magnet.

OZMA and BETSY:

The Love Magnet!

RUGGEDO:

Yes. I must regain it in order to secure Polychrome's love.

OZMA:

I wish I had it. You would be welcome to it, Ruggedo. But cheer up. You may win Polly without the Love Magnet.

RUGGEDO:

I'm afraid not. I'm a rough fellow, hard as my own metal.

BETSY:

Your temper needs pressing with a flat-iron. It's got too many crimps in it.

RUGGEDO: *(Pointing to TIK-TOK)*

What have you there?

BETSY: *(Sniffing)*

It's—it's—the remains of my dear defunct Tik-Tok. He fought a duel with the Shaggy Man over me. When Shaggy punched him, he blew to bits. I picked him up piece by piece.

OZMA:

Did you love the Clockwork Man, Betsy?

BETSY:

Yes, Ozma! Now, when he's beyond repair, I've discovered how nice he was. Oh, dear Tik-Tok! How much I'd give to be able to wind you up again!

RUGGEDO:

I know all about metal men, being the Metal Monarch, and I remember that Tik-Tok was made in my own workshop by his inventors.

BETSY:

Oh, was he?

RUGGEDO:

Yes. But he refused to obey my orders and so I threw him down a well.

BETSY:

Oh, Ruggedo, do put Tik-Tok together—and I'll give you a—a kiss, even if it gags me!

RUGGEDO:

All I want is the Love Magnet.

BETSY:

Well, I'll give you the Love Magnet, then, after Tik-Tok's put together again.

RUGGEDO:

Very good. It won't take long to do the job.

(RUGGEDO restores TIK-TOK.)

TIK-TOK:

Ma-ny thanks.

94

ACT TWO, SCENE THREE

BETSY:

Oh, Tik-Tok, I'm so glad! *(Handing Love Magnet to RUGGEDO)* Here's your reward, Ruggedo—the Love Magnet!

(Exit OZMA, BETSY and HANK.)

RUGGEDO:

Good. Now sweet Polychrome must be mine! When I do find her, the Love Magnet will win her heart.

Musical Number 24 – "So Do I!" – TIK-TOK and RUGGEDO

TIK-TOK and (RUGGEDO)

I know a lovely cross-eyed girl,
With freckles on her cheeks, (So do I!)
Her nose is red, her eyes are green,
She stutters when she speaks, (So do I!)
No living man, however gay,
Would care to lead my girl astray;
I know that she'll be true alway— (So do I!) So do I!

The whole world loves a lover, (So do I!) So do I! (So do I!)
It don't care a rap for the heart-free chap,
But adores the mushy guy— (So do I!)
The world is as cold as ice, I'm told,
It don't feed no one pie;
But the lovesick gink makes it wink, I think— (So do I!) So do I! (So do I!)

RUGGEDO and (TIK-TOK)

My millions never make me proud,
The simplest eats I buy; (So do I!)
Though squab and lobster I could have,
I choose a round steak fry; (So do I!)

95

I freely lend to ev'ry friend,
For that's an easy way to spend,
But to shave myself I condescend (So do I!) So do I!

I love the rich and haughty (So do I!) So do I! (So do I!)
I'd hate to be killed by a street car guy,
By an auto let me die! (Me, oh my!)
With kings and queens I might hobnob,
But yet I pass 'em by,
For I belong to the common mob, (So do I!) So do I! (So do I!)

(ENTER SHAGGY.)

(SHAGGY sees TIK-TOK and begins to tremble, showing excessive fear.)

RUGGEDO:

What's the matter, Shaggy Man?

SHAGGY: *(pointing at TIK-TOK and falling to knees)*
A—a—ghost! Avaunt, thou spirit of the demolished Tik-Tok—avaunt!

TIK-TOK:

Down on your knees, de-struc-tive mor-tal! *(SHAGGY hesitates, still glaring and trembling.)* Or I'll ex-plode a-gain and blow you to at-oms! *(SHAGGY kneels.)* Now beg my par-don!

RUGGEDO:

Better obey, Shaggy Man.

SHAGGY:

I—I—I beg your g-g-ghostly pardon!

TIK-TOK:

Grant-ed. Now stand up and be-have your-self!

ACT TWO, SCENE THREE

SHAGGY:

What! You're not a ghost?

RUGGEDO:

Copper ghosts are im-possible!

TIK-TOK:

Bet-sy saved the pie-ces and the Met-al Mon-arch put me to-geth-er a-gain.

SHAGGY: (Stands up, relieved)

Then I'm not a murderer? I thought it was all over for you.

*　　*　　*　　*　　*

(The following dialogue and song "One! Two! Three! All Over" are optional. They may be omitted from performance by skipping ahead to the stage direction following the next row of asterisks.)

SHAGGY: (continued)

Reminds me of one time I thought it was all over for me.

MUSICAL NUMBER 24-B - "ONE! TWO! THREE! ALL OVER" - SHAGGY and TIK-TOK with RUGGEDO

SHAGGY:

The hall was packed when I was backed
To fight the Jersey wonder.
Amid a shout I hurried out
To simply give him thunder.
One round we sparred, when something hard
Collided with me grimly.
There was a yell, and as I fell
I heard a voice say dimly:

RUGGEDO:

One, two, three,

SHAGGY:

Oh, hear the birdies singing—

RUGGEDO:

Four, five, six!

SHAGGY:

Sweet vesper bells are ringing.
I thought I heard the angels wing
Above the fields of clover.

RUGGEDO:

Seven, eight, nine, ten!

SHAGGY:

All over!

TIK-TOK

A foolish lad an auto had
And in it went a-speeding.
It stopped near town and he got down
To see just what was needing.
Cigar in teeth, he crawled beneath,
The gasoline to smell-o—
A spark, a flash, an awful crash,
And, oh, that poor young fellow!

RUGGEDO:

One, two, three!

ACT TWO, SCENE THREE

TIK-TOK:

He heard the birdies singing,

RUGGEDO:

Four, five, six!

TIK-TOK:

Sweet vesper bells were ringing.
He seemed to hear the angels wing
Above the fields of clover.

RUGGEDO:

Seven, eight, nine, ten!

SHAGGY and TIK-TOK:

All over!

(End of optional dialogue and song.)

*   *   *   *   *

(ENTER ANN.)

ANN:

Say, Shaggy, if I had the Love Magnet, would you love me?

SHAGGY:

Sure, old relic; I couldn't help it!

ANN:

Ruggedo, let me take the Magnet. I've got to have some man or I'll die an old maid!

ACT TWO, SCENE THREE

SHAGGY: *(Hastily)*

Don't you do it, Rug!

RUGGEDO:

Why, it would be a fitting punishment for all the trouble you've caused me. *(To ANN)* Will you give it back, Ann, whenever I demand it?

ANN:

Of course I will!

RUGGEDO:

Then take it—and I wish you joy! *(Hands her Love Magnet.)*

(Exit RUGGEDO and TIK-TOK.)

SHAGGY: *(Starts to run.)*

Help! Help!

ANN: *(Holding up Magnet)*
You're caught, Shaggy! There's no escape!

SHAGGY: *(Approaching her)*

Beautiful vision!

ANN:

Ah, ha!

SHAGGY:

I adore thee! Thou art the prize of my heart—

ANN: *(Tittering)*

Tee, hee, hee!

ACT TWO, SCENE THREE

SHAGGY:

The light of my life—

ANN:

Tee-hee-hee-hee!

SHAGGY:

The comfort of my soul and the joy of my waking dreams! Be mine!

ANN: *(Throws herself on him and clutches him tightly)*
I'll be your gold-mine!

MUSICAL NUMBER 25 – "THE WALTZ SCREAM" – ANN and SHAGGY

ANN:
Wherever you go you will find, as you know,
Ev'ry body is crazy to waltz;
You clinch and get busy
And whirl till you're dizzy;
There's nothing the soul so exalts!

SHAGGY:

With a girl in your arms
Whom no pressure alarms
You will seem in a dream of delight;
So you hunch and you glide
And you trip and you slide
In the way that they say is polite.

BOTH:

Ow-wow! the waltz is a rapture,
'Twill capture the great and the small;

Ow-wow! Say, ain't it amazing
How crazing it is to us all?
Ow-wow! Now as we go prancing
And dancing all over the hall,
We pant and we stagger
But try to look swagger
And waltz without halts till we fall!

SHAGGY:

Oh, my! How does it seem, girl,
To whirl till you're daffy with glee?
My eye! Ain't it a dream, girl,
To snuggle up closer to me?

ANN:

Fie-fie! There's never a cocktail
Of joy like this waltz, you'll agree,
The world will admire us,
Its plaudits inspire us
To act like two fools

BOTH:

As we be.

(ENTER *TIK-TOK, RUGGEDO, POLYCHROME, BETSY, HANK, and OFFI-CERS of the ARMY OF OOGABOO.*)

SHAGGY: (*Aside to TIK-TOK*)

Ann's a big gun in Oogaboo. I'll take her home, have her enameled and padded, and she won't be so bad to look at, after all.

TIK-TOK:

You might do worse.

SHAGGY:

Show me how, and I'm game to do it. *(To RUGGEDO.)* But where's my brother, Ruggy?

RUGGEDO:

I nearly forgot him. *(Pushes button on Magic Belt. Bell rings and IMPS Enter.)* Liberate the Ugly Man and command his presence here.

(IMPS Exit.)

(Enter a MESSENGER from the Rose Kingdom.)

RUGGEDO:

Ha! Where do you come from?

MESSENGER:

From the Rose Kingdom, Your Majesty. I am sent by the subjects of the Princess Ozma to invite her to return and rule over them.

(Enter OZMA and FILES.)

OZMA:

Why do they ask this?

MESSENGER:

They picked a Prince after you left, but he had so many thorns, he led the roses a prickly life. So they planted him and now ask you to return.

OZMA:

Here is my answer, Messenger. Return to the Roses and tell them I have found a better Kingdom to rule—the Kingdom of Love—in which my own dear Private Files is the king!

ACT TWO, SCENE THREE

ALL:

Bravo, Ozma!

(MESSENGER bows and Exits.)

(Enter UGLY MAN, led by IMPS. The UGLY MAN wears a large, ragged handkerchief tied around his head. Except for two eye-holes cut in the fabric, it completely conceals his face from everyone, including the audience.)

UGLY MAN:

Shags, whatcher doin' here?

SHAGGY:

Oh, my dearly-beloved, long lost brother! Let me see that charming face again!

UGLY MAN:

Shut up, Shags, ye durned fool!

SHAGGY:

Ah, that kindly, gentle voice! Those tender, loving words! We've come to save you, dear brother. *(Tries to embrace UGLY, but UGLY—keeping his face hidden—kicks SHAGGY in shins.)*

UGLY MAN:

Too late! No one can rescue me now. Do you know what they've done to me? I am so repulsive that when I look in a mirror I frighten myself.

SHAGGY:

Poor brother! But I beg you now to face us, who are your friends. None here will laugh or jeer, no matter how unhandsome you may be.

UGLY MAN:

I cannot face strangers, ugly as I am.

104

ACT TWO, SCENE THREE

SHAGGY:

Brother, the Metal Monarch has granted you your freedom.

UGLY MAN:

I dread to go back to the world in this direful condition. Unless I remain masked forever, my dreadful face would curdle all the milk and stop all the clocks.

TIK-TOK: *(covering his eyes with his hands in alarm)*
He'd ru-in my—z-z-z-z-z—ma-chin-er-y.

SHAGGY: *(explaining sarcastically to UGLY MAN)*
Something stops *his* clock every few minutes.

TIK-TOK:

Don't blame me, blame the—z-z-z-z-z-z-z—pat-en-tee!

SHAGGY:

(To UGLY MAN) Never mind, dear brother. I'm very happy to have found you again, although I may never see your face.

BETSY: *(to RUGGEDO)*
See here, Ruggedo, can't the enchantment be broken in some way?

RUGGEDO:

I never took the trouble to learn just how to break the charm I cast over Shaggy's brother.

POLYCHROME:

Every charm has its antidote. If you knew this charm of ugliness, Ruggedo, you must have known how to dispel it.

RUGGEDO:

If I did, I—I've forgotten.

ACT TWO, SCENE THREE

SHAGGY:

Try to think!

RUGGEDO:

I've a faint recollection that there was one thing that would break the charm.

BETSY:

We won't stand for any nonsense, Ruggedo. If you know what's good for yourself, you'll think of that charm!

RUGGEDO:

I seem to remember, dimly, that a certain kind of kiss will break the charm of ugliness.

BETSY:

What kind of a kiss?

RUGGEDO:

Why, it was—it was—it was either the kiss of a mortal maid, or—or—the kiss of a mortal maid who had once been a fairy, or—or the kiss of one who is still a fairy. I can't remember which. But of course no maid, mortal or fairy, would ever consent to kiss a person so ugly—so dreadfully, fearfully, terribly ugly—as Shaggy's brother.

BETSY:

I'm not so sure of that. I'm a mortal maid, and if it is my kiss that will break this awful charm, I—I'll do it!

SHAGGY:

That is awfully kind of you, Betsy!

BETSY:

Well, it surely won't kill me, and if it makes you and your brother happy, I'm willing to take some chances.

(BETSY closes her eyes. The UGLY MAN pushes aside the handkerchief just far enough for BETSY to kiss him on the cheek with a resounding smack.)

BETSY:

There! It didn't hurt a bit!

SHAGGY:

Tell me, dear brother, is the charm broken?

UGLY MAN:

I don't know. It may be, or it may not be. I cannot tell.

BETSY:

Let Ruggedo look at your brother's face, while we all turn our backs. Ruggedo made your brother ugly, so I guess he can stand the horror of looking at him, if the charm isn't broken.

(All turn away from UGLY MAN, except RUGGEDO, who looks behind the UGLY MAN's handkerchief. He shudders and turns away.)

RUGGEDO:

Ugly as ever! So it wasn't the kiss of a mortal maid after all.

OZMA:

Let me try. I am a mortal maid who was once a fairy, until I was exiled from my kingdom. Perhaps my kiss will break the charm.

(FILES shows some reluctance to let OZMA kiss the UGLY MAN. But she crosses to UGLY MAN and, with eyes closed, kisses him resoundingly on the cheek. RUGGEDO looks behind the handkerchief and turns away with a shudder.)

RUGGEDO:

No, that didn't break the charm, either. It must be the kiss of a fairy that is required—or else my memory has failed me altogether.

ACT TWO, SCENE THREE

BETSY:

Polly, won't you try?

POLYCHROME:

Of course I will! I've never kissed a mortal man, but I'll do it to please our faithful Shaggy Man, whose unselfish affection for his ugly brother deserves to be rewarded.

(The UGLY MAN moves his handkerchief slightly aside. POLYCHROME, with eyes closed, kisses him on the cheek.)

UGLY MAN:

Oh, thank you! Thank you! I've changed this time, I know. I can feel it! *(UGLY MAN pulls the handkerchief off, letting all see his face.)* Shaggy, I am myself again!

(ALL joyfully crowd around the UGLY MAN, patting him on the shoulders, congratulating him, etc.)

SHAGGY:

You are no longer ugly, dear brother; but, to be frank, the face that belongs to you is no more handsome than it ought to be.

BETSY:

I think he's rather good looking.

(The Rainbow appears.)

POLYCHROME:

Father! Father! *(POLYCHROME ascends to the Rainbow. She turns to look back at others, waves.)* Good-bye!

(ALL wave to POLYCHROME in return. POLYCHROME remains within sight on the Rainbow until the end of the scene.)

ACT TWO, SCENE THREE

ALL:

Good-bye!

BETSY: *(To RUGGEDO)*

Your Majesty, Polychrome has returned to her Rainbow. She said you may worship her from a distance, but she will never again return to the earth.

RUGGEDO:

Woe—woe—woe is me! But never mind. I'd no business to fool with love. I'll go back to my workshop and forget the Rainbow Girl. It's just my luck. Every one here seems happily mated but me.

BETSY:

And me! Tik-Tok says he'll be mine, but that he can't love me because he's a machine.

RUGGEDO:

I'll fix that. *(To ANN.)* Give me the Love Magnet, Ann; you don't need it now.

(ANN hands the Love Magnet to RUGGEDO. He opens a trap door in TIK-TOK and drops the Magnet in. Jingling of metal is heard.)

TIK-TOK:

Now I'm all right, Bet-sy, and I'll love you like a-ny-thing. A man is known by his works, and I'll work for you a-lone!

BETSY:

Oh, Tik-Tok, I'm so glad! Glory Hallelujah!

TIK-TOK:

You're right ac-cord-ing to my ma-chin-er-y.

ACT TWO, SCENE THREE

MUSICAL NUMBER 26 – "THE MAGNET OF LOVE" Reprise (Chorus) – ALL

BETSY:

'Tis the wonderful Magnet of Love,
It's a charm from the fairies above.

TIK-TOK:

So you can't get away from its magical sway,
It holds you a captive, object as you may.

ALL:

It is folly its pow'r to resist
When it gives all your heart strings a twist
For you'll "bill" and you'll "coo,"
Like a daft turtle dove,
'Neath the charm of the Magnet of Love!

THE END

SCENES WITH SETS AND PROPS

PRELUDE – STORM AT SEA
    Set: stormy sea backdrop, waves
    Props: model ship, model of Betsy and Hank in chicken coop

ACT ONE

SCENE 1 – THE ROSE KINGDOM
    Set: Rose Garden backdrop, Royal Rose Bush
    Props: apples, asbestos letter, rule book, Love Magnet
SCENE 2 – CROSS ROADS
    Set: countryside backdrop, Rainbow, well
    Props: hoop skirt, dead cat, toy mule, key for clockwork
SCENE 3 - FIELD OF FLOWERS
    Set: field with wildflowers backdrop

ACT TWO

SCENE 1 – CAVERN OF METAL MONARCH
    Set: rocky underground cavern backdrop, rock formations
    Props: Magic Belt, anvils and hammers, swords and shields for Imps
SCENE 2 - CAVES AND CHASM
    Set: underground caves overlooking chasm, opening for Rainbow
SCENE 2 – METAL FOREST
    Set: backdrop of Metal Trees. black area for Tik-Tok's restoration, Rainbow
    Props: handkerchiefs for Betsy and Shaggy

Sounds
    Prelude; Act 2, Scene 2 – thunder for storms
    Act 1, Scene 1 – crash of breaking glass
    Act 2, Scene 1 - roar of furnace, crash of tin mine caving in
    Act 2, Scenes 1 and 3 – bell ring for Magic Belt
    Act 2, Scene 3 – jingling of Love Magnet inside Tik-Tok

This list is provided as a guide and may be customized according to the needs and capacities of a particular production.

MUSICAL NUMBERS BY CHARACTER

SHAGGY MAN
"An Apple's the Cause of It All"
"The Clockwork Man"
"Act One Finale"
"Rainbow Bride"
"Folly!"
"One! Two! Three! All Over"
"The Waltz Scream"
"The Magnet of Love" Reprise

BETSY
"The Magnet of Love"
"The Clockwork Man"
"Dear Old Hank"
"Act One Finale"
"Rainbow Bride"
"Folly!"
"The Magnet of Love" Reprise

OZMA
"There's a Mate in This Big World for You"
"Ask the Flowers to Tell You"
"Act One Finale"
"Oh! Take Me"
"Just For Fun"
"The Magnet of Love" Reprise

POLYCHROME
"Oh! My Bow"
"I Want To Be Somebody's Girlie"
"Act One Finale"
"When in Trouble Come to Papa"
"Rainbow Bride"
"The Magnet of Love" Reprise

TIK-TOK
"The Clockwork Man"
"Act One Finale"
"Rainbow Bride"
"Folly!"
"So Do I!"
"One! Two! Three! All Over"
"The Magnet of Love" Reprise

QUEEN ANN OF OOGABOO
"The Army of Oogaboo"
"Act One Finale"
"Fight for Oogaboo"
"Rainbow Bride"
"The Waltz Scream"
"Magnet of Love" Reprise

PRIVATE FILES
"The Army of Oogaboo"
"Ask the Flowers to Tell You"
"Act One Finale"
"My Wonderful Dream Girl"
"Oh Take Me"
"Just For Fun"
"Magnet of Love" Reprise

RUGGEDO
"Work, Lads, Work"
"When in Trouble Come to Papa"
"Rainbow Bride"
"Forgotten"
"So Do I!"
"One! Two! Three! All Over"
"The Magnet of Love" Reprise

UGLY MAN
"The Magnet of Love" Reprise

ARMY OF OOGABOO
"The Army of Oogaboo"
"Fight for Oogaboo"
"The Magnet of Love" Reprise

FIELD FLOWERS
"Act One Finale"

METAL IMPS
"Work, Lads, Work"
"The Magnet of Love" Reprise